Sacramento

A Pictorial History of California's Capital

12/05/82

Harry;
No matter how long
we stay in Sacramento
or what happens to you &
me, I felt this was a
book you'd enjoy having.
Merry Christmas ! I love you.
Ann

Sacramento

A Pictorial History of California's Capital.

by Julie Elizabeth Mims and Kevin Michael Mims

Design by Jamie Backus Raynor

The Donning Company/Publishers
Virginia Beach, Virginia

Special thanks to Kathe Waterbury for the beautiful cover drawing of California's State Capitol.

Library of Congress Cataloging in Publication Data:

Mims, Julie Elizabeth, 1949-
   Sacramento.

   Bibliography: p.
   Includes index.
   1. Sacramento, Calif.—Description—Views.
2.   Sacramento, Calif.—History—Pictorial works.
I. Title.
F869.S12D65   979.4'54   80-27520
ISBN 0-89865-120-4 (pbk.)

Dedicated with love to Eleanor, Andrea, Mary Ann, and Oliver;
and also to Mary Bisharat,
who held our marriage together while we held this book together.

Contents

Foreword 9

Preface 11

Chapter 1
The Valley and Its People 13

Chapter 2
1830-1860 17
    The '49ers 20
    Pony Express 36
    The Railroad 39

Chapter 3
1860-1910 47
    The Capitol 48
    The Riverboats 51
    The State Fair 92

Chapter 4
1910-1981 113

Bibliography 205

Index 206

HOUSE OF REPRESENTATIVES

Foreword

In this vivid book, Julie and Kevin Mims have told a success story of the kind America has produced over and over again—the birth, growth, struggles and flourishing of California's capital city. But the story is not told in highwinded historical passages; instead, we see it in the faces of Sacramentans, how they looked and how they lived.

The miners' stories are revealed in their weathered faces and roughened hands, a more telling biography than words alone could provide. Rather than being subjected to laborious monologues on Victorian society, we are there with those who practiced that lifestyle; we are inside the Stanford game room, we attend a Crocker gala, we are part of the opulence and can see its splendor for ourselves. Technology's rapid rise is told in photos which show the stunning contrast between old and new. Pictures of horse-drawn carriages beneath high tension wires, and breathtaking biplanes swirling above lazy riverboats illustrate how progress and history are interwoven in the magic tapestry of the present. The Mimses have let Sacramento tell its own story and have brought history to life.

Robert I. Matsui

Robert Matsui
Member of Congress

The sight of an approaching Pony Express rider must have been breathtaking to those fortunate enough to observe horse and rider seemingly fly across the terrain. This wiry yet delicate, hardy yet graceful horse was the Spanish Barb. He carried the all-important mail in locked saddlebags from St. Joseph to Sacramento. This magnificent horse arrived in the Americas around 1492 and survived quite well on this continent, through the years developing stamina and resistance to the elements. He was well qualified to carry the skilled riders of the Pony Express.

Preface

This pictorial history of Sacramento was a labor of love to write and assemble. At times it was an utterly frustrating assignment. Nevertheless, the end result is a book emphasizing the people who have been the foundation of this beautiful city since its beginning so long ago.

Most of this publication is devoted to yesteryear, to the formative years of this capital city. The last portion deals with current means of preserving and displaying the past. The citizens of Sacramento and various agencies have realized the importance of historical preservation; however, much of the city has already fallen victim to the wrecking ball and the elements.

All photographs, with the exception of the present-day group, are from the Museum and History Commission Collection.

All reprinting of photographs was beautifully done by McCurry's Photo Lab. Many thanks to Chloe and Hope for their much-needed help; it was a pleasure working with them.

And, our thanks to Barry Cassidy, president of the Sacramento County Historical Society, for the opportunity to write a pictorial history of the city of Sacramento.

Sacramento River

"And some of us have swept around snow-walled curves of the Pacific Railroad in that vicinity, six thousand feet above the sea, and looked down as the birds do, upon the deathless Summer of the Sacramento Valley, with its fruitful fields, its feathery foliage, its silver streams, all slumbering in the mellow haze of its enchanted atmosphere, and all infinitely softened and spiritualized by distance—a dreamy, exquisite glimpse of fairyland." (Mark Twain, Roughing It).

Chapter 1

The Valley and Its People

The Sacramento Valley rests between two distinguished and regal mountain ranges, the Sierra Nevadas on the east and the Pacific Coast range on the west. This beautifully diversified terrain was years in the making. During the ice age, a glacier most likely etched a huge gorge between these two (at the time unstable) mountain ranges. This 1,000-foot-deep crevasse was slowly and methodically filled with silt and sediment of the ages and in time formed the valley floor as it appears today. Earthquakes tossed and tumbled the giant region, gradually forming the unique terrain of the present.

The valley exhibits an astounding diversity. Lush green deltas abruptly give way to rolling foothills. The green grasses and colorful wildflowers disappear rapidly at the onset of summer, leaving a golden beige landscape dotted with massive oak trees. The region is well suited for agriculture due to these geological factors and also to the atmospheric conditions. Hot summers and mild winters make this valley a veritable paradise for growing. This vast region surrounds the "City of the Plain," the city of Sacramento.

Sacramento is located at the confluence of two rivers, the Sacramento and the American. It is surrounded on the south by the delta, and to the east are the foothills of the Sierras. North and west are mainly farming regions that make the outlying areas profitable to agriculture, one of the largest enterprises in the state.

Yet before Anglo invasion of this area, other peoples lived and toiled in the valley. They were the Maidu Indians, a branch of the Valley Nisenan group.

The Maidu Indian's domain covered over 10,000 square miles, which included the Sacramento area. Their language or dialect was separated into three parts as were their ecological provinces; these separations were labelled mountain, foothill, and valley. The Maidus were peaceful people with 100 to 110 inhabitants per village. Pole and brush homes were most common and many were subterranean dwellings banked with soil.

The Indians of California, due to geographical formations, were isolated from foreign contact for a much longer period than has been seen in various other groups. The mountains formed a natural barrier to distant travel and contact with outside groups.

The Sacramento and American rivers were the main sources of food for the local Indian tribes.

This crude drawing of an early house in the Sacramento Valley depicts a rambling ranchstyle home on a wide expanse of land.

GEN. JOHN A. SUTTER.

For John A. Sutter, the title "Captain" was complimentary. Born Johann Augustus Sutter in the Black Forest town of Kandern, Bavaria, he lived for a time in Switzerland, becoming an apprentice bookseller at the age of sixteen and a clerk for a clock merchant and grocer at nineteen. Sutter's inability to find a profitable way to make a living may have contributed to his fascination with the New World. In 1834, he booked passage to America, hoping for success. One of Sutter's dreams was to found a magnificent city, a New Helvetia, a haven for Europeans in the barbaric frontier. He ultimately traveled a roundabout route to California, incorporating side trips to the Sandwich islands, Alaska, and the Willamette Valley of Oregon. He entered the American River at its confluence with the Sacramento in 1839, and on a grassy knoll not far from the river, Sutter found the site for his long-dreamed-of empire. In 1847, John Sutter began construction of a sawmill and at the same time gave material form to his dream.

Chapter 2
1830-1860

In the Spanish-Mexican period of California's development, Anglo-American infiltration became more and more of a problem for the peaceful Maidu. The first of this group were the fur trapping mountain men who were generally hostile toward the Indians of the Sacramento area. Sacramento was named in 1808 by Gabriel Moraga, a Spanish explorer who named the valley for the Holy Sacrament, a Christian religious rite. In contrast, the few settlers in this region in the 1830s and 1840s lived in a basically co-existent atmosphere with their native neighbors. In the early days of settlement, Mexican authorities were well aware of the explorations in the interior valley surrounding Sacramento, yet initially did not feel compelled to limit Anglo expansion.

Of all the foreign and Anglo explorers, trappers, or settlers, the most important to this region was Johann Augustus Sutter, who was born in Bavaria.

At Yerba Buena (San Francisco) in 1839, Sutter was given a cool reception and his request for a grant of land was denied; subsequently, he was sent to Monterey to appear before the Mexican authorities to plead for land. Mexico was just beginning to resent and fear the advancement of others into California.

Mexican Governor Alvarado told Sutter to explore the river and valley regions of the Northern California area and take command of eleven Spanish leagues, seventy-six square miles, that were to his liking. Alvarado was looking for self-gain, also. He needed an outpost in the north to keep in touch with the area and the Indians but did not wish to put his manpower in such outlying areas.

Sutter commanded a small party to San Francisco, then up the Sacramento River, which was a feat in itself. It took him eight days to find the true entrance to the river. On August 12, 1839, Sutter entered the American River at its confluence with the Sacramento. Upon his arrival, he viewed a valley generally without trees except for the groves of oak and cottonwoods gracing the river banks. It was this scarcity of wood for lumber that led to one of the most important incidents in California history. In August of 1847, Sutter began construction of a sawmill forty miles east of Sacramento at Coloma on the American River. This mill would enable him to sell lumber to the steadily arriving immigrants.

The discovery of gold a few months later brought an influx of people from all corners of the world. Sacramento became a major supply and commercial center for miners, who could buy their provisions at inflated prices from merchants in the rapidly growing, prospering town.

Although Sacramento was growing at a rapid rate, tragedy befell the city time and time again. Fire and flood leveled the majority of the buildings many times in the first few years. Wooden buildings as well as a general lack of caution concerning torches and oil lamps contributed to the fire hazards.

Flooding was a geographical problem which could not be changed. As the rivers rose, the city streets became muddy rivers while small boats maneuvered to rescue stranded inhabitants in second-story windows. Yet, miraculously, this city continued to be built and rebuilt with never-wavering confidence. Sacramento would survive despite the wrath of the rivers.

John Sutter's son, John A. Sutter, Jr., actually founded the city of Sacramento. In 1848, he hired topographical engineer William H. Warner to draft the official plat of the city. "Evidently Warner was an orderly person, for he made the simplest and best plan for Sacramento City—thirty-one north and south streets to be numbered in order from the embarcadero; twenty-six east and west streets named for the letters of the alphabet" (Lord, A Sacramento Saga).

And survive it did. The people of this city struggled and banded together to form citizens' committees, councils, and other organizations to deal with the varied problems. Sacramento became a real home to the adventurous newcomers, not merely a stopover for the mines. Energy was placed in building and expansion.

Resident merchants were becoming wealthy from sales to miners, and freight companies were kept busy trekking into the mountains to supply the camps. Transport of goods to the gold regions was no easy task. Soon the valley floor rose to hills and then to steep cliffs and rocky, narrow passages. Most of the mines were located in isolated areas, and mule teams pulled thousands of pounds of food and equipment per day into the mines. Merchants soon realized that a faster and more efficient method was needed. New wagons were built, more mules were added to each team, and—surprisingly enough—camels were imported for pack use by some enterprising entrepreneurs. But all of these methods proved inefficient. Until this time, the most effective and modern means of shipping goods east of the Mississippi was the railroad. This was the innovation California needed.

Sacramento has reigned as capital city of California from the year 1854 by law, yet it did not hold that honor physically until January 1, 1855. The capital of California had several homes, including Monterey and San Jose. However, the mayor of Sacramento and the council offered the governor of California, also a Sacramentan, use of the courthouse and also a prime piece of real estate for the construction of a permanent building to house the state government. It was an offer too good to refuse. Despite an intense fire in 1854 which leveled nearly all of the city, a new building was finished in record time to be the site of state government. However, negotiations were underway to purchase a larger piece of land, one worthy of the great state of California, and build a grand capitol building. Despite the deep financial stress of the state government, construction was begun in 1861 of a new building which would rival the White House in grandeur. The California State Capitol in Sacramento has been the seat of government for 125 years.

Sacramento City, 1849. Already, commerce has turned to the banks of the Sacramento River and away from Sutter's Fort.

The first building constructed on the site was made from adobe brick and used as Sutter's residence. Later, a blacksmith shop, carpenter shop, storeroom, guestrooms, saloon, and mill room were added. Walls of adobe surrounded these structures to provide the best security.

"It emerged, the fort, as a wilderness outpost, as a point of security for travel in an otherwise untamed land. It stood for something more. It stood as a testament to the fact that development of the vast interior of this abundantly rich valley was inevitable." (Severson, Sacramento: An Illustrated History).

The '49ers

While making a routine inspection, James W. Marshall, superintendent of mill construction at Coloma, made his historic discovery of gold in January 1848. Marshall was sent to Coloma (fifty miles east of Sacramento) to oversee the work being done at Sutter's Mill, which would soon supply the steadily arriving immigrants to John Sutter's "New Helvetia" with lumber for their homes and stores.

Sutter's Mill at Coloma developed into an important mining site, producing riches by the ounce rather than by the board foot.

News of the discovery traveled fast thanks to men like Sam Brannan, a Mormon from New York. Brannan, as well as many others, was skeptical about this great discovery. He traveled to Sacramento in April of 1848, met with Sutter, and visited the site at Coloma. This opportunist was back on the streets of San Francisco by mid-May, waving samples of the gold over his head and shouting the good news. Within weeks the great migration had begun.

Gold! Gold! Gold!—January 24, 1848—James W. Marshall's cursory inspection of the millrace unearthed the precious metal that would change California's destiny rapidly and drastically.

Within months began a migration from all corners of the world to partake of the wealth that was sure to be had by all. By 1849, news had traveled far and wide. The influx of miners arrived mainly by ship at the docks in San Francisco, then charted a course up the Sacramento River by steamboat, then on to the mines heavily laden with supplies.

All this preoccupation with gold and newfound wealth overshadowed a boom of another kind. Sacramento, the fledgling city, was teeming with merchants getting exhorbitant prices for goods. Sacramento of the 1850s was a city trying its wings in a frontier region. It boasted one of the first real hotels in California and also the Eagle Theatre, which was the first building erected in California for use solely as an entertainment center.

By day, mule teams hauled wagons from the embarcadero to the mining regions, and stores provided provisions for miners on horseback as well as on foot.

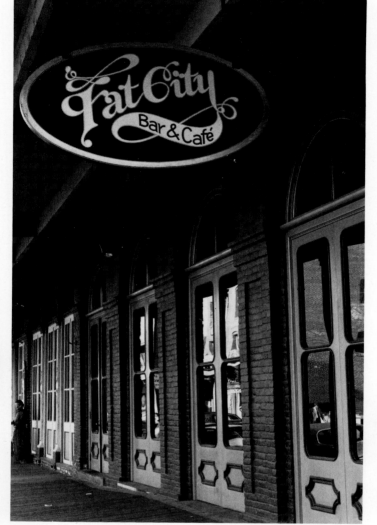

Chinese miners were not a common sight during the Gold Rush. Racial persecution made it difficult for the Chinese to prosper in California's early days. Today, there are many successful Chinese businesses and business men. Frank Fat is the owner of some of Sacramento's most popular restaurants, including Fat City and China Camp in Old Sacramento.

MINERS' VARIETY STORE.

No. 64 J st., ~~above~~ *below* 3d st.,
Sacramento City.

W. R. PRINCE has constantly on hand the following articles, at the lowest wholesale and retail prices, and will supply Miners and teams for all the mines with implements of every description necessary for their use. GROCERIES, PROVISIONS, and LIQUORS, of all kinds, of the very best quality, put up in proper sized parcels for teams and pack mules. In the assortment are the following goods, viz:

Quicksilver, Retorts, Rockers, Crowbars, Picks, AMES' best Shovels, and others. Camp Kettles, Camp Stoves, and all other cooking utensils, Axes, Hatchets, Handles, and Tools of all kinds. Rifles, Guns, COLT'S REVOLVERS, and other Pistols. Whip, Wood, and other Saws. Spikes, Nails, and Tacks of all sizes, with a great variety of Hardware and Cutlery. Tinware, Crockery Earthen, Stone, and Glassware.— Powder, Balls, and Shot of all sizes. Caps, Flasks, Shot Bags. Magnets, Wash-pans, Miners' Spoons.

Trowels, Scythes and Sneaths, Scythe Stones and Rifles, Hay Forks, Rakes. Garden Seeds of all kinds. Gold Scales of all kinds, and sets of Gold Weights, Counter Scales, Platform Scales, Scale Beams, Spring Balances, and other Scales and Weights of all kinds. Brass, Pewter, and Wood Faucets. Dinner Bells, Mule and Cow Bells. Rope, Twine, Sail, and other Needles, and Palms. Medicine Chests. Bees-wax, Sealing-wax, Letter and Wrapping Paper, Pens, Ink, Stands, Pencils, Blank Books and Stationary. Bar, Hoop, and Rod Iron, Steel in Bars. Clothing, Blankets, Calicoes, Canvass, Duck, Drilling, Ticking, Toweling, Hats, and Caps. Gold and Silver Lever and Hunting Watches, Gold Pens and Pencils. Boots and Shoes, Sole and Upper Leather, Chamois Skins, Gold bags. Corks, Oil Cloth, India Rubber Goods. Tar, Pitch, sperm and Olive Oil, soap, Candles, starch. Saleratus, Cream of Tartar, seidlitz powders, Stoughton's bitters, sarsaparilla syrup. China and other Preserves, Pickles, Flour, Pork, beef, bacon, Hams, Mackerel, salmon, Oysters, Lobsters, sardines, Eggs, Coffee, Tea, sugar, Molasses, Chocolate, butter, Lard, Cheese, Rice, Corn Meal, spices of all kinds, Figs, Raisins, Dried Fruits, Hops, Chile beans, Potatoes, Onions, seed Wheat, Indian corn, barley, split Peas. Beads for Indians, Dominoes, backgammon boards, American and French cards. Brooms, Tobacco, segars. Harness, Riding and Pack saddles, bridles, Hobbles, Whips, &c.; Fiddles and strings; Mexican and American spurs; Knives and Forks, Pocket Knives, Bowie Knives, butts and screws, Locks, bridles and bits, stirrups. Belts and sheaths; Rope of all sizes, bed cords, Umbrellas; Iron Pumps, Lead Pipe, and all other desirable articles.

Placer Times' Press.

Sarsaparilla syrup, backgammon boards, and beads for Indians are among the many items offered by the Miners' Variety Store in this advertisement. Of course other, more useful goods such as gold scales and medicine chests are among the numerous supplies listed here.

Believe it or not, this is what the average easterner thought a typical miner would look like while on his way to his daily diggings. It would seem the folks back east were aware of all of the items necessary for working a claim except perhaps the most important—the pack mule.

The "Long Tom" was a popular method of mining gold during the early stages of the Gold Rush. Inside the "Long Tom" were wooden ridges spaced apart in even intervals. Paydirt was poured into the "Long Tom" and spread evenly over the ridged base board; then the miners used buckets of water to wash away the dirt and lighter sediments while any particles of gold would settle behind the ridges since they were too heavy to wash away.

MINERS WASHING THEIR GOLD EARTH THROUGH THE "LONG TOM"—A SCENE NEAR SACRAMENTO, CALIFORNIA.

With all of their money and with few other means of amusement, it was perhaps inevitable that miners took to gambling with a heartiness they applied to practically nothing else other than working their claims. This drawing could easily be a scene from one of the many vignettes of the gold rush days by Bret Harte ("The Outcasts of Poker Flat," "The Luck of Roaring Camp"), who chronicled the lives and times of the '49ers.

A miner receives a shave while another grizzled prospector awaits his turn.

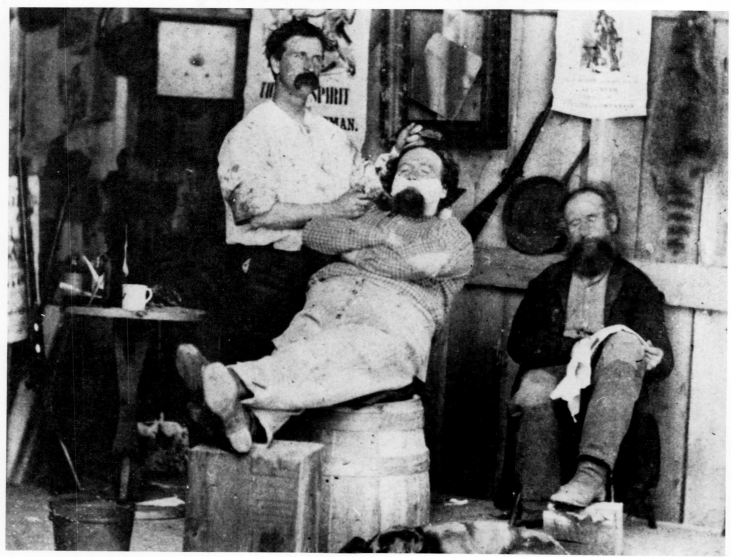

"The Adams Express Company was located on Second Street in 1852 when this picture was taken. The company was the first to link the mines to the Atlantic seaboard, but it failed in the panic of 1855 after spirited competition with Wells Fargo" (Severson, Sacramento: An Illustrated History).

In classic '49er form, these miners stand well prepared for their journey into the hills to search for gold.

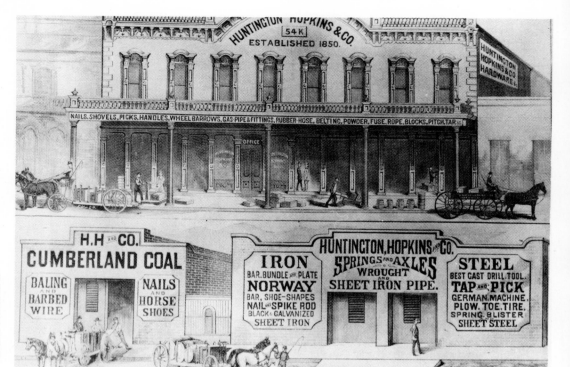

This lithograph depicts the Huntington Hopkins hardware store, established in 1850. Both Huntington and Hopkins were members of the "Big Four"— founders of the Central Pacific Railroad. This view also shows the Cumberland Coal Company next door.

According to Thor Severson (Sacramento: An Illustrated History), "The site of the first agricultural fair was Warren's New England Seed Store on J between Front and Second."

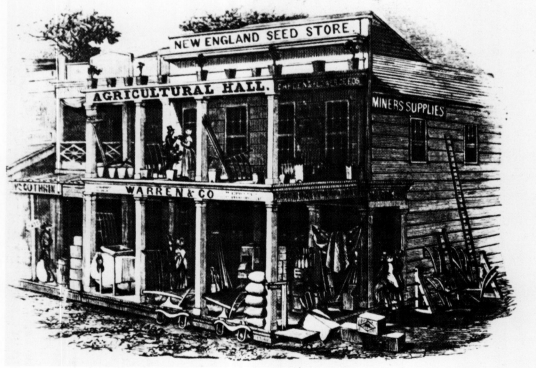

Hold-up men perched in the perilous peaks along the stage route through the Sierra Mountains and preyed upon the coaches heading east of Sacramento. Inevitably, it became mandatory that stagecoaches carry at least one armed guard for protection against ambush by bandits such as Charles E. Boles, a San Francisco socialite known as the notorious "Black Bart."

28

OVERLAND MAIL ROUTE
TO CALIFORNIA.

Through in Six Days to Sacramento!

CONNECTING WITH THE DAILY STAGES
To all the Interior Mining Towns in Northern California and Southern Oregon.
Ticketed through from PORTLAND, by the

OREGON LINE OF STAGE COACHES!

And the Rail Road from Oroville to Sacramento,

Passing through Oregon City, Salem, Albany, Corvallis, Eugene City, Oakland, Winchester, Roseburg, Canyonville, Jacksonville, and in California— Yreka, Trinity Centre, Shasta, Red Bluff, Tehama, Chico, Oroville, Marysville to SACRAMENTO.

TRAVELERS AVOID RISK of OCEAN TRAVEL

Pass through the HEART OF OREGON—the Valleys of Rogue River, Umpqua and Willamette.

This portion of the Pacific Slope embraces the most BEAUTIFUL and attractive, as well as some of the most BOLD, GRAND and PICTUERESQUE SCENERY on the Continent. The highest snow-capped mountains, (Mt. HOOD, Mt. SHASTA and others.) deepest ravines and most beautiful valleys.

Stages stop over one night at JACKSONVILLE and YREKA, for passengers to rest. Passengers will be permitted to lay over at any point, and resume their seats at pleasure, any time within one month.

FARE THROUGH, FIFTY DOLLARS.

Ticket Office at Arrigoni's Hotel, Portland.

H. W. CORBETT & Co.,

PORTLAND July 19, 1866.   Proprietors Oregon Stage Line.

Boasting of six-day service and "pictueresque" scenery, H.W. Corbett's Oregon stage line advertisement warns travelers of the riskiness of ocean travel while making no mention of the many potential hazards which occasionally dogged stage passengers, such as a breakdown of either man or beast due to the hostile terrain of "some of the most beautiful and attractive scenery on the continent."

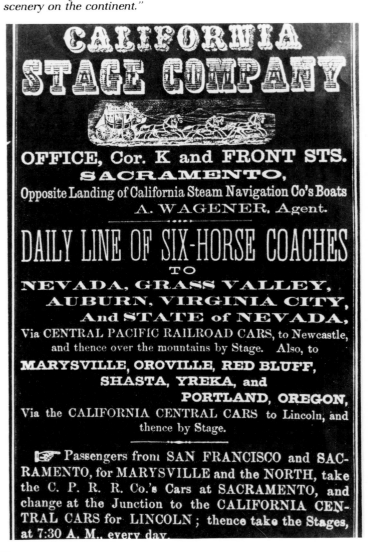

The California Stage Company also advertised daily transportation to all points north, as far as Portland, Oregon.

This is a lithograph of a California Stage Company coach.

The La Grange, Sacramento's prison ship. This strange vessel was brought into service around 1850 and used as the only city jail until it sank in the flood of 1862.

This lithograph of "the great inundation" of 1850 shows the fledgling city of Sacramento coping with a flood, an ever-present danger when living near two winter-swollen rivers.

The John Bruener Company sold little more than wagon wheels and barrels in 1853. By 1856, it had evolved into a full-service furniture store providing for the needs of Sacramento residents.

The first store of Weinstock and Lubin was located at Fourth and K streets. Like other modern stores, this began as a general store catering to miners and later to permanent residents. Today, Weinstock's is a department store chain with branches throughout California, Nevada, and Utah.

J Street circa 1860 is reminiscent of a scene from a Western movie. The blurring of moving wagons and horses gives this photo an eerie quality.

Sacramento was deluged by rampant rivers in 1862.

By 1865, Bruener's had expanded into one of the city's largest companies. No longer content to supply only mining provisions, Bruener now engaged in household goods and furniture.

"Anthony Egl fled the revolutions in Hungary in 1848. When he arrived in Sacramento in 1855, he already was a naturalized citizen. His wholesale fruit, nuts, and confections business on J Street prospered. So, in 1860, he built the two-story brick home at 917 G Street" (Vanishing Victorians)

A Wells Fargo Express wagon was a familiar sight in downtown Sacramento for many years from the 1850s until the twentieth century. This man was a letter and small parcel carrier in the downtown area.

This house at 925 G Street was built by A. A. VanVoorhies, in the late 1850s. He was "the finest type of cultured pioneer." "The Prince," as he was called, owned a harness factory in Sacramento which employed 100 men and crafted various leather goods (Vanishing Victorians).

The great immigration of Chinese people in the early 1860s mandated the construction of a house of worship for the new arrivals. It was the first Chinese Baptist chapel erected in the United States and stood on the northwest corner of Sixth and H streets. Construction funds were raised by the Southern Baptists of Virginia and to a lesser extent by local Chinese citizens. Today, the site is occupied by the Southern Pacific Railroad yards.

Initially a wooden structure, today St. Francis Catholic Church and Convent School is a large stone edifice covering nearly the entire block. A 2,000-pound bell which arrived in Sacramento on July 13, 1859, has enhanced both buildings. Since that time, scores of Sacramentans have been moved by the solemn ringing of this pioneer bell.

St. Rose of Lima Catholic Church loomed high above the surrounding structures at Seventh and K streets. St. Rose was demolished in the late 1800s, making way for a new stone structure housing the United States Post Office. Today, the site is occupied by a small park.

34

Cathedral of the Blessed Sacrament Catholic Church on J Street. A century ago this building was a towering structure which dwarfed the surrounding buildings.

Pony Express

ALEXANDER MAJORS
OF RUSSELL MAJORS AND WADDELL

Alexander Majors was a co-founder of the Pony Express along with William Russell and W. B. Waddell. The first rider from St. Joseph, Missouri, arrived on April 13, 1860, and was escorted from Sutter's Fort into town by a throng of residents. Horse and rider received a vigorous ovation from awaiting onlookers when they arrived at Second and J Street with their load of eighty letters. Relay stations ten to twenty-five miles apart, 500 horses, and eighty young men were responsible for the new rapid mail service over every terrain imaginable. Mark Twain describes the Pony Express rider in Roughing It: "He rode fifty miles without stopping, by daylight, moonlight, starlight, or through the blackness of darkness—just as it happened. He rode a splendid horse that was born for a racer and fed and lodged like a gentleman; kept him at his utmost speed for ten miles, and then, as he came crashing up to the station where stood two men holding fast a fresh, impatient steed, the transfer of rider and mail-bag was made in the twinkling of an eye, and away flew the eager pair and were out of sight before the spectator could get hardly the ghost of a look.

"The stage-coach traveled about a hundred to a hundred twenty-five miles a day (twenty-four hours), the pony-rider about two hundred and fifty. There were about eighty pony-riders in the saddle all the time, night and day, stretching in a long, scattering procession from Missouri to California, forty flying eastward, and forty toward the west, and among them making four hundred gallant horses earn a stirring livelihood and see a deal of scenery every single day in the year."

The Pony Express was in operation for only eighteen months, pushed aside by the new transcontinental telegraph. Yet few can forget the adventurous riders and hearty horses of that daring undertaking.

The Pony Express statue at the corner of Second and J streets in Old Sacramento commemorates the arrival of horse, rider, and mail at the Hastings Building across the street.

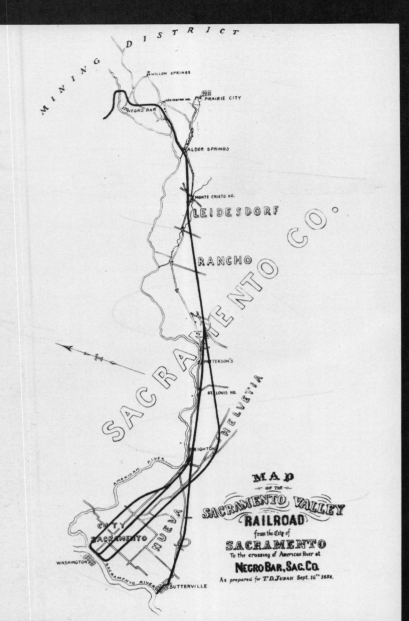

MINING DISTRICT

WILLOW SPRINGS

LEXINGTON HO. PRAIRIE CITY

NEGRO BAR

ALDER SPRINGS

MONTE CRISTO HO.

LEIDESDORF

RANCHO

SACRAMENTO CO.

PATTERSON'S

ST. LOUIS HO.

HELVETIA

BRIGHTON

AMERICAN RIVER

CITY
SACRAMENTO

NUEVA

WASHINGTON

SACRAMENTO RIVER

SUTTERVILLE

MAP
OF THE
SACRAMENTO VALLEY
RAILROAD
from the City of
SACRAMENTO
To the crossing of American River at
NEGRO BAR, SAC. CO.
As prepared for T. D. JUDAH Sept. 16th 1854.

This 1854 map shows the Sacramento Valley railroad line, stretching twenty-two miles from Sacramento to Negro Bar. This short but historic line was engineered by T. D. Judah, who later was instrumental in the foundation of the transcontinental railroad.

Bloomer Cut was the first major obstacle encountered by Central Pacific workers as they attempted to build a railway heading east out of Sacramento into the Sierra Mountain range. Bloomer Cut is just east of Sacramento.

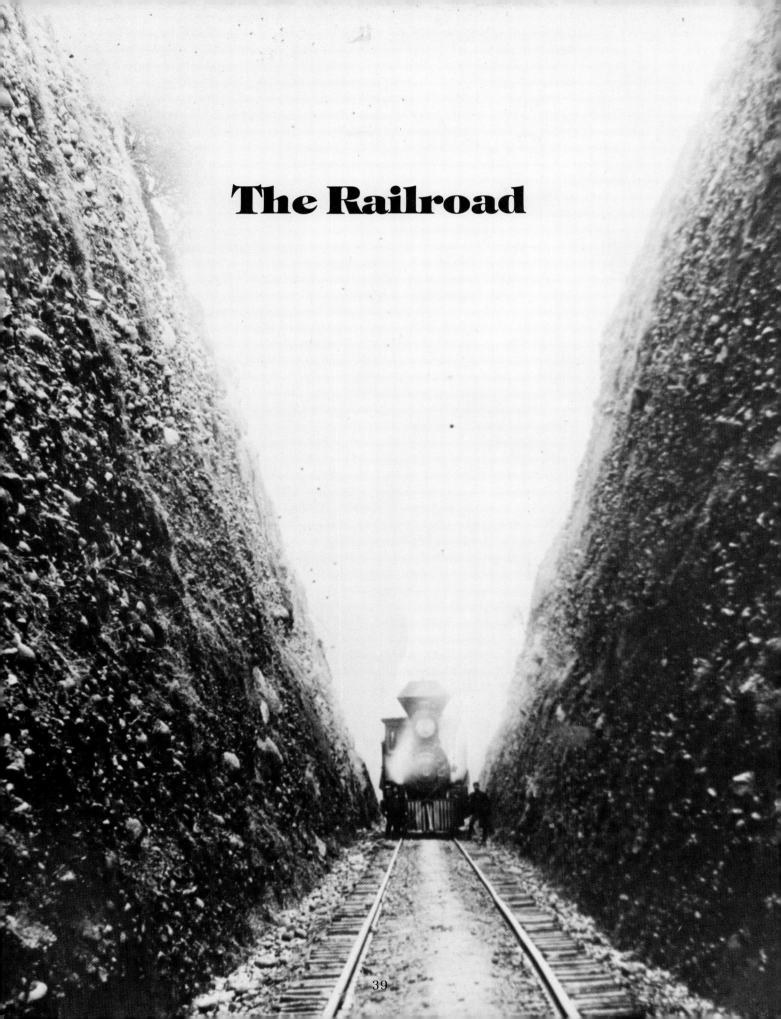

The Railroad

Governor Leland Stanford

At first, a western railroad was desired only as a convenient way to ship to the mines. The first line was laid from Sacramento to Folsom, a distance of twenty-two miles at a cost exceeding one million dollars.

Theodore D. Judah was hired to survey and engineer the construction of the line. A brilliant surveyor who proposed the course for this historic line, he became instrumental in the construction of the transcontinental railroad and in the formation of the Central Pacific Railroad.

Construction of the Central Pacific Railroad over the Sierras began in 1863 from the Sacramento embarcadero. It was a dream of a small group of Sacramento businessmen, including four men who built it into one of the largest monopolies the state has ever known. The Big Four—Collis P. Huntington, Mark Hopkins, Charles Crocker, and Governor Leland

Mark Hopkins

Collis P. Huntington

Stanford—were initially private investors in the scheme to build a railroad over the Sierras. Judah was persuasive, promising positions on the board if these businessmen would invest. He even traveled to Washington to seek financial help from the government, but the onset of the Civil War made the offer seem anything but promising to officials in the east. However, private backing was enough, and construction began. It was agonizingly slow until hardworking Chinese laborers were hired. They made up the majority of the railroad crew and were instrumental in laying the tracks over the most difficult terrain of the Sierra Mountain range. The line was completed from the West and the East in 1869. The two laboring engines met at Promontory, Utah, amidst a hero's welcome. The Central Pacific became a huge conglomerate.

Charles Crocker

East meets West in this depiction of the historic junction of the Central Pacific and Union Pacific railroads at Promontory, Utah, on May 10, 1869. Here, a golden spike was driven into the ground and a telegram immediately sent to Sacramento with one word—"done".

The locomotive Governor Stanford arrived in Sacramento aboard the schooner Artful Dodger on October 5, 1863. It was initially built in Philadelphia, dissassembled and shipped to San Francisco, and finally arrived in the city of Sacramento. This photo was taken about 1865.

The first depot for the Central Pacific Railroad was designed by Collis P. Huntington and built at the foot of K Street in the winter of 1863. This building was also used as the first ticket office for the then-beginning company. Built in one day, it cost $150. The site is now a parking lot.

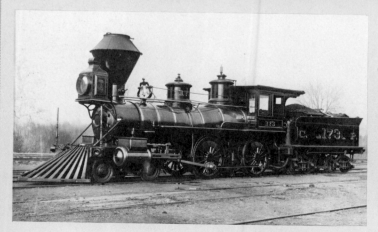 

Central Pacific Railroad locomotive engines.

A memorial statue of A. J. Stevens is located in Plaza Park at Ninth and J streets. Stevens arrived in Sacramento in 1870 to work for the Central Pacific Railroad as a general master mechanic, but he was most famous for his innovations in construction and redesign of locomotives. He rebuilt many for the company during the 1870s and patented several inventions. Stevens' popularity with the railroad workers was signified by the granite statue erected in his honor in 1889.

The finished capitol building was a grand sight. In the late nineteenth and early twentieth centuries, the grounds were open and spacious. In 1981, they are covered with soaring trees and tall shrubbery. The site is surrounded now by buildings which dwarf its height, and the majestic dome seems to have diminished beside the stark office buildings of the 1980s.

Chapter 3
1860-1910

Sacramento fell and thrived, flourished and floundered through its formative years. The West was the land of dreams and miracles to many men and women who came to find a better way of life. It is remarkable to reflect on the progress that was made from the time of the great rush for gold in 1849 and 1850 until 1870, when Sacramento was a grand capital city with all the trimmings. Beautiful structures, lush gardens, and fine furnishings brought a more cultured aspect to this once rowdy town.

Sacramento was a city full of contradiction. The electric railway made its debut on Major Street in 1887, bringing outlying areas into the limelight for residential purposes. The new freedom of movement in Sacramento brought about many major changes. One of the most visible was the demise of the corner store which had previously been a necessity in each neighborhood. Larger department stores were opening in the downtown area and attracting shoppers from the outer county.

Although technology proved hazardous to some old-fashioned businesses, generally it was a much welcomed addition to daily life. The late 1800s saw the advent of the steam-propelled tractor, of great importance to agricultural industry but merely a precursor of a new, more modern convenience.

The introduction of the auto in Sacramento occured at a street fair in 1900. Citizens were amazed to see a vehicle running on something other than real horse power. This car intrigued and frightened spectators, who regarded it either as the boon of the future or a new fangled nuisance. Nevertheless, the first automobile agency opened its doors in 1903, and state registration of all cars followed in 1905. In fact, by the onset of World War I, horses were heavily outnumbered by the motor car, and motor-driven trucks had even sent the familiar freight wagon into permanent retirement.

Sacramento's residents were always sure of the opportunities available here, and it was their stubborn resolve to make this town inhabitable, under the most adverse of conditions, that cemented the deep roots of civic commitment. These settlers and miners who came in the early months of the gold rush and stayed to live and work after the boom subsided are the basis of the city today.

Within forty years of its founding on the banks of the Sacramento River, the city of Sacramento had become one of the most important cities in the United States.

The Capitol

This is a lithograph of the Sacramento County Courthouse which housed various state offices for a short time (1855-1856). However, it was not large enough to function adequately. In the spring of 1856, a $300,000 bond issue was passed to build a suitably spacious structure, but construction was halted by state officials and the land returned to the city. It was another four years before a new site was found and purchased. The state capitol stands on these city blocks today.

For years, Sacramento was regarded as a city doomed to be buried under water for much of the year, so in the 1860s the task of raising the buildings with jack screws began. By the 1870s, half the city had been raised approximately twelve feet, saving it from disastrous flooding. Here workers undertake the strenuous task of raising the courthouse.

These two photos show the state capitol during construction. The first, taken from the top of the uncompleted structure, looks down upon the building's excavation site and its residential neighbors. Construction began in February of 1861. Eight years later, after contending with floods and the crippling Civil War, the capitol building was ready for occupancy in December 1869.

As their handiwork nears its completion, members of the capitol construction crew take time out from their labors to pose for this informal picture.

The state capitol groundskeepers, circa 1870. These gentlemen were responsible for the complete maintenance of lawns, gardens, fountains, and trees.

The Riverboats

Although this photo of four grand riverboats steaming down the Sacramento River was a staged scene for the movie Dixie, starring Bing Crosby, it could easily have been an actual race. Steamboat captains were notorious for engaging in wild and sometimes dangerous speed contests from San Francisco upriver to Sacramento.

Riverboats were vital to commerce in Sacramento in the days following the Gold Rush. These huge vessels were the swiftest and most efficient method of transporting passengers and goods to and from the San Francisco Bay area. They carried lumber, dry goods, livestock, and passengers more quickly than any other means at that time. Rival companies vied for business by offering reduced rates and more services to waiting customers.

CABIN S: DECK \
CHRYSOPOLIS & YOSEMITE
PACIFIC RAIL ROAD DEPOT

This circa 1860 photo of the Sacramento embarcadero shows the steamer Chrysopolis waiting at the dock. "Chryssy," owned by the California Steam Navigation Company, was the fastest riverboat on the Sacramento River with a record time of five hours and nineteen minutes from Sacramento to San Francisco.

Most of the fastest boats were owned by the California Steam Navigation Company, but rival companies were fiercely competitive. One such rival was Captain Kidd, skipper of the Washoe. Determined to set a new speed record at any cost (ultimately the cost was the loss of at least fifty-four lives), Kidd challenged many C.S.N.Co. boats including the Yosemite and the Antelope, but his most fateful adversary was the Chrysopolis.

On September 5, 1864, the Washoe left San Francisco a few minutes behind the Antelope and the Chrysopolis. Determined to overtake them, Captain Kidd employed reckless tactics. His engine crew ran the boiler pressure up to 135 pounds although 100 pounds would have been sufficient. The Washoe easily overtook the cumbersome Antelope, but was still forty-five minutes behind "Chryssy" at the halfway point, Rio Vista. After leaving Rio Vista, the Washoe entered the winding waters of Steamboat Slough, but the combination of too much speed and too much pressure was a deadly duo. When the boat listed sharply to navigate a tight turn, the water in the boilers washed to one side, exposing the superheated flue (a rod which heats the water and builds the pressure inside the boilers). The intense heat of the naked flue, which should have been immersed in water, was too much for the metal boilers. The Washoe erupted in a hideous explosion, decimating the ship and killing dozens of people.

Ironically, the site of the disaster was just seven miles from the watery grave of the Nevada, another vessel which had met her death at the hands of Captain Kidd. She had gone down one year earlier while racing another C.S.N.Co. craft, the New World.

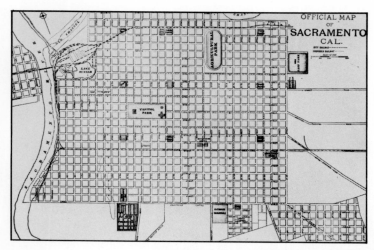

The city of Sacramento and surrounding area, circa 1870.

The Opposition Steamship Line was a rival of the California Steam Navigation Company. Dock workers pose in front of the storage shed for the steamer Chin Du Wan.

The Apache *was owned by the California Steam Navigation Company.*

This barge is bound for Sacramento loaded with iron and steel products for the Thomson-Diggs Company.

The Sacramento embarcadero looking north toward the I Street bridge, about 1870.

The Delta King, shown here, and the Delta Queen were the pride of the river in the 1920s and 1930s. They ferried passengers to and from San Francisco for more than a dozen years prior to World War II. However, they were taken out of service at the onset of the war and have gone their separate ways. The Queen is on the Mississippi again. On the other hand, the King has spent years decomposing in the Delta. San Francisco Bay area investors have purchased this once-proud riverboat and are in the process of refitting it to its original glory.

The Sacramento embarcadero as seen from the Yolo County side of the river, about 1920.

56

The proprietor of the Glen Dairy poses with his rig, circa 1880. This business was located at the corner of Thirty-Eighth and E streets.

Streetcar employees pose with one of their trolleys.

This is an interior view of a provisions store located in the community of Consumnes, south of Sacramento City.

As in many cities in the United States, local breweries began shutting their doors when advanced transportation methods made it possible to conveniently ship beer from those areas whose natural elements (abundant spring water and choice hops) afforded them the best of breweries. Ruhstaller's City Brewery was located at Twelfth and H streets.

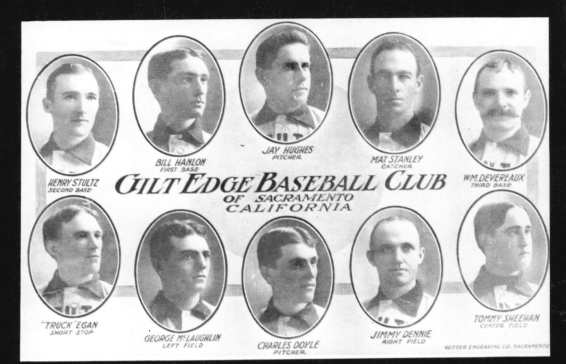

GILT EDGE BASEBALL CLUB OF SACRAMENTO CALIFORNIA

HENRY STULTZ
SECOND BASE

BILL HANLON
FIRST BASE

JAY HUGHES
PITCHER

MAT STANLEY
CATCHER

WM. DEVEREAUX
THIRD BASE

"TRUCK" EGAN
SHORT STOP

GEORGE McLAUGHLIN
LEFT FIELD

CHARLES DOYLE
PITCHER

JIMMY DENNIE
RIGHT FIELD

TOMMY SHEEHAN
CENTER FIELD

SUTTER ENGRAVING CO., SACRAMENTO

Sacramento hosted many sports teams. One of these was the Gilt Edge Baseball Club sponsored by the Ruhstaller City Brewery, makers of Gilt Edge Beer. (This is their team photo in 1896 when they were state champions.)

Employees of two local breweries seem proud of their profession in these staged portraits. The demand for good beer and the bountiful supply of hops from the outlying areas made breweries a significant industry in Sacramento.

Interior and exterior shots of the "Old Corner" bar with proprietor William Ellsworth.

Stable owner J. M. Nielsen rented horses and rigs by the day, week, or month, and all were guaranteed to be as sound and trustworthy as the sleek animal posing here with a stablehand.

Executives of the Pacific Mutual Life Insurance Company pose at the counter in their front office in this circa 1890 photo. As Sacramento and the rest of the country moved into the twentieth century, more and more men chose to work at the white collar office jobs rather than in the factories or fields.

The interior of the Pioneer Telegraph Building at 1015 Second Street. Today it houses a popular gift shop in Sacramento's Old Town area.

This interior of an early drug store shows diverse merchandise: from plasters to skull caps to candy and perfume.

These interior photos of Noacks Jewelry Store and an unidentified drug store (with scale) typify the long, narrow floor plan of most downtown structures. These corridor-like business establishments were necessitated by the mere twenty-foot width of many downtown parcels. (It has not been determined whether the vicious bulldog in the drug store photo was used to encourage customers to keep their accounts current.)

These men are the proprietors of the Y Street Dairy.

S. H. Farley's was one of the most successful grocery stores of the era, offering three delivery wagons for better service.

Oak Park evolved into a popular residential area and became one of Sacramento's first suburbs with the onset of streetcar lines. This new form of transportation made commuting a reality for businessmen and shoppers.

This photo of the Anspach Mule Company and a stagecoach being pulled by eight mules was taken just a few years ago, probably taken during a parade, but it is reminiscent of those splendid days when everyone traveled by coach or horseback. The Anspach Mule Company was located at Thirtieth and R streets.

The corner grocery offered all goods and services needed by residents in the immediate area. The proprietors usually lived upstairs.

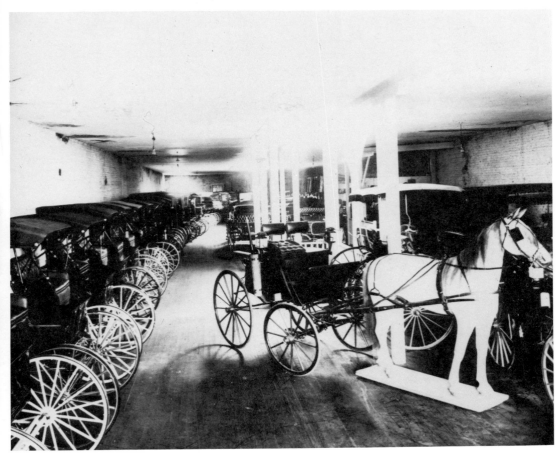

Carriage travel was for the elite, and Sacramento's many factories supplied numerous models varying in size and price range.

These handsome horses are patiently waiting to begin their day's work pulling the Wells Fargo and Company Express wagon.

Agriculture is the major source of income in California, and the fertile farmlands surrounding Sacramento are important to the statewide industry. These mule wagons are hauling hops to the local breweries.

Victorian architecture relied heavily upon scrollwork and "gingerbread."

Modern technology affects even the farmer. By 1890, technology had finally advanced farming equipment, which for centuries had relied simply on the sweat and muscle of man and beast.

This regal Victorian structure was the residence of Governor Leland Stanford. Standing at the corner of Eighth and N streets, it was a hallmark in early Sacramento to exhibit the distinctive Mansard roof. (The building still stands and is now a home for wayward girls.)

Governor Stanford's wife and children enjoyed billiards in the game room of their home in the 1870s. Even ladies were allowed to play such manly games in the privacy of their own homes.

Victorian splendor and ostentatious display were important to the wealthy residents of Sacramento. Delicate lace and sturdy wood complement each other in this elegant bedroom.

This magnificent Victorian was the home of Charles Crocker, co-founder of the Central Pacific Railroad. It was located at the corner of Eighth and F streets, and like so many others it is gone and all but forgotten.

This house was designed by Seth Babson and James Seadler in 1882. It was owned by Llewellyn Williams, who sold it in 1891 for $30,000 in gold. It has changed hands several times and withstood a move to the lot next door. In 1907, H. Edward Yardley transformed this residence into a funeral home. Today the building is owned by Morey Holmes and is available for social gatherings.

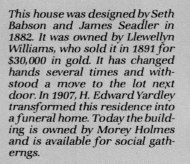

This early photo of the Governor's Mansion depicts the classical architecture of the nineteenth century's opulence and grandeur. This beautiful white building was owned by Albert Gallatin, designed by N. D. Goodell, a noted Northern California architect, and constructed in 1877 by Uriah Reese.

Gallatin arrived in Sacramento in 1861 and was soon employed in the Huntington Hopkins hardware store as a porter and later a salesman. After a brief stay in Nevada, Gallatin returned to Sacramento and Huntington Hopkins. By 1888, he was president of the company.

Gallatin resided in this house for ten years, then moved to San Francisco. Joseph Steffens, the father of noted author Lincoln Steffens, purchased the property at Sixteenth and H streets, where he lived until 1903.

Until 1903, there had never been a permanent residence for California's governor. Many houses had been considered, then rejected for one reason or another. The Capitol Commission agreed to purchase the Steffens house for $32,500. Thus, this stately private residence became home to California's first family until the Reagan administration in 1967. Then it was declared hazardous, lacking in fire escapes and other safety features.

Today, tours are conducted daily by the California State Park and Recreation employees.

Albert Gallatin

The Sisters of Mercy Hospital was located at Twenty-Third and R streets. This area is now occu-pied by residences and ware-houses.

The Pioneer Society, founded in 1849, awaits the arrival of President Grant in front of their headquarters on Seventh Street. The society is a patriotic organization founded by some of the original "'49ers" and is still in existence today.

The Central Pacific Hospital was located at Thirteenth and C streets and provided for the well-being of Central Pacific Railroad workers.

The Bell Conservatory was located on 7 acres covering W, X, Y and 7th and 8th streets in Sacramento. It was a gigantic greenhouse with exhibits of native as well as tropical flora Margaret Crocker built at a cost of $20,000. An identical structure in San Francisco's Golden Gate Park attracts hundreds of visitors daily. It is a shame that Sacramentans are deprived of this beautiful greenhouse today. The conservatory was razed at the turn of the century.

The Buffalo Brewery was located at 21st and Q streets in Sacramento. It covered almost three full blocks and provided the city with perhaps the best and most popular brew. Today, this site is the home of the Sacramento Bee, one of the two major newspapers in this city.

Company I of the second regiment infantry displays weapons and strength in this 1863 photo of Sacramento's contribution to Civil War preparedness.

Fourth of July cannon salutes were a popular displays of patriotism. This one took place near Capitol Park, around 1880.

A picnic in the country on a sunny afternoon was typical Victorian entertainment for Sacramentans.

Oak Park School, circa 1900.

Like all Americans, Sacramentans love a parade.

A young violinist tunes her instrument.

This musical duo appears prepared either to entertain an outdoor gathering or maybe just to enjoy playing some familiar tunes in the backyard.

Portrait of an unidentified Sacramento family.

A wide-eyed child poses for her first studio portrait.

This group of men exemplifies men's fashions in the late nineteenth century. They were members of the "Old Leakers" Baseball Club.

A class portrait from the Union Primary School, circa 1900.

Orangevale is situated in the northeast part of Sacramento County and was once nothing but groves of oranges for as far as the eye could see. Today, most of the orange groves have given way to subdivisions and commercial properties, and Orangevale is now a thriving community.

High water—always inconvenient and sometimes a deadly peril. Sacramento is located at the confluence of two unpredictable rivers and therefore fell prey to the elements before the network of levees was built.

The Golden Eagle Dairy, owned by Marty and Brothers, was located on Land Drive in Sacramento. They served fresh dairy products to the residents of the southern portion of the city. Tony Marty is pictured behind the fence.

Picnickers at a get-together.

The Rhoads School opened its doors in May of 1872. After a one and one-half month term, certificates were awarded to most of the twenty-one students. The school was built with private funds yet operated under the jurisdiction of the Sacramento County Common School District. The school was abandoned in 1949 and had varied functions until restoration in 1976. On May 19 of that year it was moved to Elk Grove Park.

The Mary J. Watson Grammar School located at Sixteenth and J streets covered an entire block which is today the site of the Sacramento Memorial Auditorium. This view is dated 1873.

This dapper gent has rented his horse-drawn rig from the popular Fashion Stables.

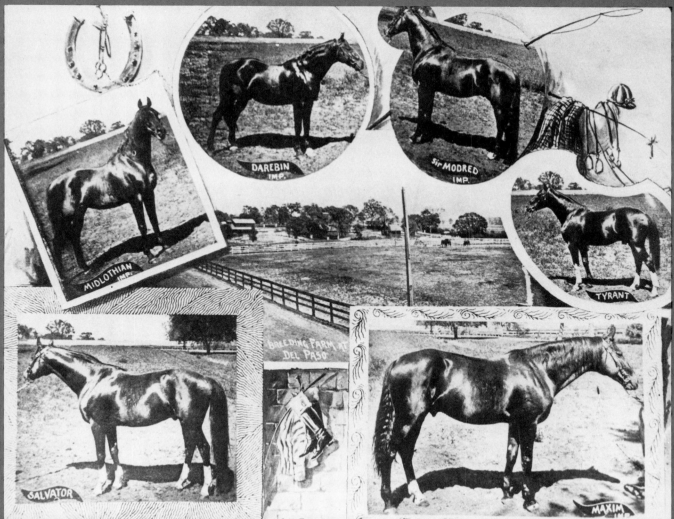

These horses were just a few of those owned by James Ben Ali Haggin and stabled on this ranch, the Rancho Del Paso. Haggin owned some of the finest thoroughbreds in the country in the 1880s. Today, the Rancho Del Paso is subdivided into residential and commercial areas covering thousands of acres north of Sacramento.

This interior of an unidentified factory office exemplifies the use of wood in construction and furnishings. Even a business office featured oak appointments in the days before plastic and aluminum decor.

The meeting room of the Masonic Lodge on J Street in Sacramento.

One of the honors of belonging to a fraternal organization was being able to play in the band. This group was the Associated Order of Foresters of America.

87

This baseball team was sponsored by the Capital City Wheelmen, a group of cycling enthusiasts. The picture was taken at the "Old Diamond" at Fourteenth and K.

National Guardsmen sit in readiness during the Pullman Strike of 1894.

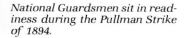

The great Pullman Strike of 1894 affected cities across the nation. Sacramento was no exception; it too lay stagnant as half the railroads in the country were crippled by striking laborers. This photo shows the first train out of Sacramento when the strike ended.

The Central Pacific Railroad depot.

Courier service between railroads and hotels was an additional convenience for travelers. Here, several horse-drawn carriages and freight wagons await the arrival of incoming passengers and goods adjacent to the Central Pacific Railroad depot, circa 1880.

This group portrait of Southern Pacific Railroad Employees was taken outside the depot around 1899.

Southern Pacific Railroad employees gather to watch the christening of a new engine, circa 1920.

The State Fair

This circa 1930 photo of the now-abandoned state fair-grounds on Stockton Boulevard shows the parade of fine horses before the grandstand.

Perhaps the best-known horse race track in the Sacramento area was the Louisiana course, located at Twelfth Avenue and Franklin Boulevard. It was built by A. G. Butler and E. M. Skaggs, well-known sporting men in the city. Construction began in 1855, and the track was the site of many exhibitions of horses and cattle. It became a popular center for races, stock shows, and festival games. Horse-drawn stage service was provided at half-hour intervals from the Orleans Hotel on Second Street. Many memorable races were run on this course in the 1850s, and one of the outstanding horses of the time, Silver Grey, was buried in the infield of the track in recognition of her speed. The Odd-Fellows Bank succeeded Skaggs in ownership of the land and eventually sold it to a farmer named Curtis. By 1892, the track was a prime piece of real estate worth a quarter of a million dollars. Today it is a residential area, Curtis Park.

The State Agricultural Pavilion was located at Sixth and M streets.

STATE AGRICULTURAL PAVILION.

94

Occident, world champion trotter in 1873, was owned by Governor Leland Stanford. His record *time of 2:16.75 was set on September 17, 1873, at the one-mile track at Union Park.*

The California State Fair began in 1852 with the formation of the California State Agricultural Society to display the state's diverse crops and varieties of livestock. With eighty members by 1854 and incorporation by the Society, the first fair was held in San Francisco with the livestock exhibition at Mission Dolores.

In 1855, Sacramento hosted the fledgling fair with exhibitions held in three places around the county; it was an inconvenient plan. Industrial exhibits were displayed at the courthouse (the home of the state capitol at the time); livestock was shown at the Louisiana Track at Twelfth and Franklin Boulevard; and the baked goods, dry goods, and entertainment were presented at the Pavilion at Sixth and M streets.

The third fair in 1856 was held in San Jose and the fourth was held in Stockton; both lasted four days. It was in Stockton in 1857 that the question of a permanent location for the fair was discussed. In 1858, with the fair held in Marysville, a new constitution was put into effect, and the fair would travel no more.

Sacramento became the permanent home of the fair by a constitutional amendment in 1861. A special city tax was collected for the purchase of property and construction of adequate facilities to house the growing exhibitions. Twenty acres of prime land were given to the Society by the Sacramento Park Association. These original city blocks (E Street, H Street, and Twentieth to Twenty-Second) became known as Union Park. One year later, six more blocks were obtained and the existing half-mile tract expanded to a full mile.

The 1860s were years of expanded exhibitions and premiums as well as financial woes and damaged grounds, yet the stock exhibits continued to increase and every county was represented with livestock from horses to cattle to rabbits.

The 1870s were a decade of improvements to the forty-three-acre fairgrounds. New stands, stalls, and sheds were erected, and the question of adequate accommodations for visiting Californians arose. A new service was provided by the Central Pacific Railroad, which agreed to transport all merchandise and livestock to and from the exhibition by rail.

The California State Fair continued through the 1890s, outgrowing its facilities at a rapid rate. Union Park was completely surrounded by residential areas, and the Pavilion could not accommodate the growing number of entrants. The twentieth century arrived, and a new site was sought for the fair. Union Park was demolished in 1905, subdivided, and renamed Boulevard Park. The fair moved to a newly purchased eighty acres on Stockton Boulevard, opening in 1906. Today, the fair is held at the modern California State Exposition grounds near the American River and Interstate 80.

The California State Fair boasts of having "something for everyone," and the 1916 State Fair even provided for those who considered a head-on train collision high entertainment.

Young Tecumseh was owned by John Peasley, owner of the What Cheer House on Front Street.

Electric lights and sewing machines were among the mechanical marvels at the 1895 State Fair, which included exhibits from most of the city's most prominent merchants. John Bruener and Weinstock Lubin and Company displayed goods at the fair to take advantage of the excellent publicity. These two photographs show The Capitol Gas Company's extravagant display and the A. J. Pommer home sewing machine demonstration. Domestic exhibits were held in the Agricultural Pavilion at Sixth and M streets.

97

These beautiful dapple gray horses pulled an oil wagon in a demonstration at the 1925 California State Fair. The motor car had replaced the faithful work horse in business and pleasure by the 1920s.

This publicity photo was made for the upcoming state fair, circa 1930. The 1930s saw a decline in attendance and entries, yet the fair continued its run through the Depression years.

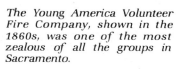

The Young America Volunteer Fire Company, shown in the 1860s, was one of the most zealous of all the groups in Sacramento.

This firehouse at Eighteenth and L streets is still in operation today.

The young city of Sacramento
was a haphazard conglomera-
tion of canvas and wood buildings—a highly flammable community illuminated by candles
and lamps.

One of the first disastrous
fires occurred in 1851 and was
soon followed by demands for
fire protection by outraged
citizens. Community concern
brought about the formation of
the Citizen's Fire Committee
that year. Later, separate hook-
and-ladder companies were
organized and situated throughout the downtown area. They
were supplied with hoses, carts,
and other "modern" firefighting
equipment. The men making up
these companies were usually
young, and for the first twenty-
two years, firefighters were
volunteers.

"A fire company with its engine house provided a sort of
club atmosphere similar to a
fraternal organization. Each
company had a number desig-
nation, a formal name, a nick-
name and a motto, as well as a
uniform of red shirt, fireman's
hat and belt with the name of
their company on it" (McGowan,
Fire! Fire!).

After ten years Sacramento
was fairly well protected with
companies manned by 400 volunteers. But, despite the close
proximity of the Sacramento
and American rivers, an adequate water supply was an im-
possibility due to the lack of any
incline to help the flow of water.
However, the city water works
building housed 240,000 gallons,
and cisterns were located
throughout the city to supply
firemen with needed water.

Dr. Joseph A. McGowan de-
scribes early firefighting in
Sacramento: "Volunteers, wher-
ever they were, stopped what
they were doing and rushed to
their fire house, donned their
fire hats and grabbed the drag
rope of the pumper and the hose
cart. Led by the Foreman with
his trumpet through which he
gave direction, they hauled their
weighty equipment in the direction of the alarm. Sometimes
they could see the flame or
smoke and proceeded directly
to the fire. On other occasions
they ran to a convenient inter-
section from which they could
see in four directions and sight
the fire, or other fire companies
which knew where the fire was
...."A general stampede was
made by the different companies in as many different
directions as no light was visible
to direct the firemen which
direction to move."

The Western Hotel's coach, circa 1900.

This photo of the John Breuner Company shows a grand three-story department store in contrast with the wood frame store of the 1860s.

Oliver, Joyce, J. Calvert, and George Marala wore typical attire of railroad employees of the early 1900s.

A City Police Patrol wagon, circa 1870.

The corner of Seventh and K streets was bustling with activity at the turn of the century. The contrast of past and present is evident in electric and gas-powered cars, horse-drawn wagons, and the streetcar rails. The towering stone structure is the U.S. Post Office.

This 1910 photo shows a small mule harvester in the fields near Sloughhouse. These harvesters were an important invention and valued by the local farmer, for whom harvesting grain became a simpler task.

The Crocker family livened up their lavish home with a flower festival, held in honor of Margaret Crocker. This photo was taken in the late 1880s.

The Crocker Art Gallery is the oldest museum in the west. Constructed in 1871 at the corner of Third and O streets, this grand structure has housed the finest art for over 100 years. Built by E. B. Crocker and his wife Margaret at a cost of $200,000 this gallery holds some of the most valuable paintings and sculpture in the country. The Crockers traveled to Europe to collect a diversified group of rare old masters and drawings. In 1885, after the death of her husband, Margaret Crocker deeded the gallery and its treasures to the city of Sacramento and the California Museum Association. Today it has undergone a complete renovation and is as beautiful as it was in the late nineteenth century.

The Central Pacific machine shops appear in the distance across Sutter's Lake (China Slough). This body of water, for years a place for mosquitoes to breed and waste to be deposited, was filled in, making way for the Southern Pacific yards in the 1920s.

The parents of Sacramentan Myrtle Johnson decorated their buggy for the city's Fourth of July celebration in 1900.

Southern Pacific employees pose for a group photo in 1899. These men were supervisors or general managers of their respective divisions.

Bicycling was and still is a favorite pastime for Sacramentans. These cyclists in the 1890s stopped for a rest along the Riverside Road, today Riverside Boulevard.

This horse waits patiently in front of the Sunset Telephone Company. Again the past meets and intermingles with the future.

Sacramento's residents moved into the twentieth century with a determination typical of this city. Technology was developing at a rapid rate with the onset of motor cars and the newest wonder of the century, air travel. Sacramentans moved in the direction of change and progress along with the rest of the nation. Residents coped with war, depression, and another war as well as numerous problems unique to Sacramento.

The new reliance on auto transportation brought investors throughout the country to buy and subdivide various outlying areas. In 1910, the 44,000-acre Rancho Del Paso which had been owned by James Ben Ali Haggin was sold to two large development companies. This beautiful land had been kept intact since 1844, when it was acquired in a Mexican land grant. This vast acreage became Rio Linda and North Sacramento.

World War I dominated the years 1914 through 1920. The devastation of war was heightened by the equally disastrous influenza epidemic of 1918. Yet, the war years brought advancement, partially due to government-financed projects.

Sacramento was the site of a small aircraft factory which was in full operation in 1917, and the following year an airfield was proposed on a 700-acre site east of the city. It was called Mather Field and used as a training center for troops.

Another well-remembered event was prohibition. On June 30, 1919, Sacramento city was considered "dry," a not altogether welcomed happening. Despite the obvious inconvenience of this new law, Prohibition had an economic impact on the Sacramento area; vineyards and hops fields which graced the county fields were pulled and the land sold.

Gold mining, never really forgotten, was booming from 1913 thru 1923. No longer was the miner kneeling in creek beds twelve hours a day or shoveling pay dirt into a "Long Tom." Now a mechanical dredge pulled dirt and minerals from the bottom of rivers and man-made ponds.

The decade of the 1920s brought a sigh of relief and a bit of relaxation to citizens. The length of women's skirts seemed important and silent movie houses flourished as Sacramento regained its composure after the war. Contentment and prosperity were short-lived, however. The "Crash of '29" and subsequent Depression beset Sacramento with gigantic problems. Unemployment was reflected by the increasing number of people residing in Hoovervilles in the years 1931 and 1932. Labor strikes merely added to the then-explosive atmosphere.

The Depression era also brought an end to steamship travel on the river. Automobile and freight hauling trucks became major methods for transporting passengers and goods.

The depression ended essentially as the threat of another war loomed large on the horizon. Prosperity returned. As always, war stimulated industry and agriculture in the Sacramento area. This pro-Roosevelt city banded together to face the unseen enemy. Communism was feared, and political radicalism was evident in many small, hastily organized groups.

Without a doubt the most appalling action in Sacramento during the war was the mandatory evacuation of Japanese-Americans. Supposedly, these hard working citizens posed a threat to national security because of the proximity of Pearl Harbor to the Califor-

nia coast. Although some compensation was paid to the returning citizens after the war and a public apology tendered, the evacuation itself was deplorable.

Post-war Sacramento again picked itself up to continue with the business at hand. Industry and agriculture slowly returned to normal production levels. The period was characterized by growth, but rapid growth has its dangers. The demise of many historic Sacramento structures was taken in stride many years ago and regarded as a necessary evil for the sake of convenience and progress. Now, however, Sacramentans have realized the mistake of demolition instead of reconstruction. Never again will we see many of the sites depicted in the photographs in this publication. If only the importance of preservation had been con-

sidered as much as fifty years ago, much of historic Sacramento might still be intact.

Because The Sacramento Redevelopment Agency has supported the preservation of the most valuable homes in the "Old City," it is now difficult to raze a structure without consent. Finally, many old homes and other buildings are relatively safe from the wrecking ball.

The 1950s, a decade not unlike the 1920s, was one of prosperity and a settled contentment. Looking toward the future was a common bond among Sacramentans, and the last twenty years of this century have been spent reflecting upon past mistakes and cultivating a new optimism for the future.

Fremont Primary School at Twenty-Fourth and N streets was photographed on June 15, 1914. The principal at this time was Miss Huntington and the teacher was Miss Richards. Today, the Fremont School is used for adult education classes but retains the charm of the early twentieth century.

Three young ladies pose in front of a covered bridge-like structure in Sloughhouse, southeast of the city, circa 1910.

The Oak Park Gateway, circa 1910.

"Joyland," an amusement park in the suburb of Oak Park, was popular with Sacramentans both young and young at heart in the 1910s. This roller coaster constructed mainly of wood provided many thrills for the stout-hearted.

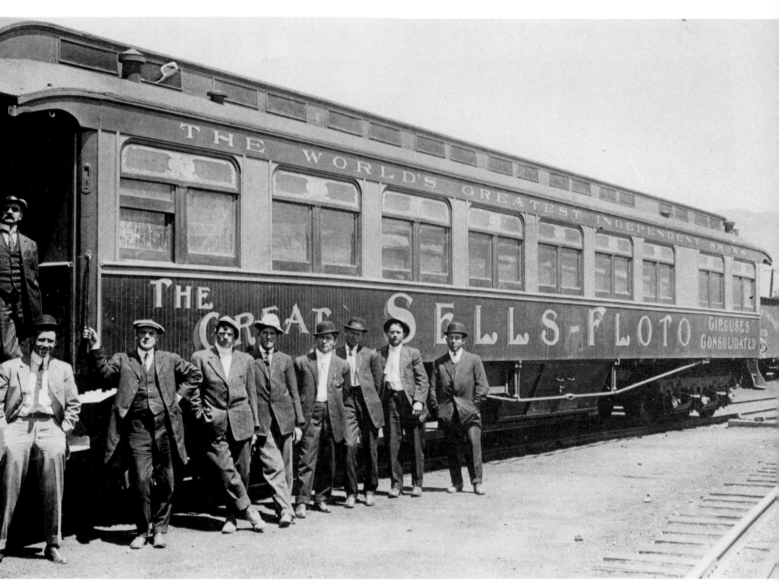

The Sells-Floto Circus, shown about 1920, was one of many to visit Sacramento during the last 100 years. This company traveled the state by train entertaining children and adults.

World War I brought about many changes in the Sacramento area. One of them was the need for women in the factories to replace the men who had gone off to war. These women were valued employees of the Southern Pacific Railroad in a time when unity was a national cause.

The 1920 senior class of Sacramento High, the oldest high school west of the Mississippi.

The Sacramento County Court-house, circa 1920.

Sacramento High School at Thirty-Ninth and Y streets.

This publicity photo for the Sacramento Union was taken in the Sierras east of Sacramento, about 1920.

This pilot appears ready to soar into the sky in his biplane. Barnstorming was not a myth, and some Sacramentans remember vividly the wild dives of the carefree flyers of the 1920s.

Airplanes were becoming a familiar sight to the residents of Sacramento in the days before the onset of World War I. This photo taken in 1916 at Mather Air Field shows a line of new biplanes constructed at the Liberty Iron Works in North Sacramento.

Everybody got into the act as flying became the rage in the 1920s.

Hops by the bale were delivered to Sacramento from the outlying areas by trucks such as the one in this 1930 photo.

The Sacramento Memorial Auditorium was erected in 1926 replacing the Mary J. Watson Grammar School. It is a beautiful brick and stone building covering an entire block. The hall holds everything from rock concerts to Roller Derby.

This circa 1920 photo is an aerial view of the northwest portion of the city. This area was almost completely commercial and has remained so to the present day.

A circa 1920 aerial view shows the site of the soon-to-be-constructed Southern Pacific Railroad depot. Building materials can be seen in the middle of the photo, stacked in readiness for the work to begin.

Work has begun at the Southern Pacific Railroad construction site.

The Southern Pacific Railroad depot at Christmas after its completion, 1926. This immense brick structure is still standing today.

"Elegant" well describes the lobby of the Senator Hotel in the 1930s. Expensive furnishings, china, silver, and linens, were purchased with the comfort of the guest in mind. Over the years, the furnishings of this once grand hotel have been stolen, vandalized, or sold to the highest bidder.

Eggs Benedict was a specialty of the Senator Hotel Coffee Shop. Residents and visitors alike enjoyed the food and service of this popular restaurant, shown about 1930.

This barber shop was located in the Senator Hotel. High officials in state government from the 1920s until the 1960s frequently crossed the street from the capitol to relax in the barber's chair. This circa-1930 photo shows an efficient and modern shop.

A lazy afternoon on the river with a backdrop befitting the Mississippi, circa 1940. This family enjoys the warm sunshine as the Delta King drifts slowly by on its way downriver to San Francisco.

This view of J Street in the 1920s includes streetcars, automobiles, and a lone cyclist in the middle of the street.

Old and new meet in this 1920 picture of a Frederick's Photo Service car in the foreground and a gold dredge somewhere along the river in the background.

The Anchor Bakery was located at 2015 J Street in downtown Sacramento. The automobile, having made its debut as a novelty, now replaced the horse and wagon as the principal mode of delivery.

A Sacramento couple in their motorcar.

21st & H Sts, Sacto

Palm trees in the middle of Twenty-First Street are the only reminders of Union Park, where the fastest horses in the state once raced. By 1920, this area was a secure residential neighborhood.

These homes on Twenty-First Street in Sacramento are located on the site of the Union Park Race Track. Union Park flourished for forty years until the State Fair was moved to the Stockton Boulevard site. These homes, built around 1910, are beautiful examples of the bungalow architecture.

The Hotel Land bar, with polish-
ed oak woodwork, gleaming
spittoons, and inlaid tile floors.

East meets West in Sacra-
mento's Chinatown area near
Third and I streets, where such
combinations as the W. and O.
Pharmacy and a Chop Suey Cafe
and dancing hall typified the
atmosphere of coexistence.

Sacramento had numerous hotels serving weary travelers. A favorite of businessmen was the Hotel St. James, which offered reasonable rates.

This is a group picture of members of the Sacramento Police Department, circa 1940. Sacramento Union columnist Kirt Mac Bride stands at left in the back row.

These photos show the Sacramento Fire Department in the 1920s.

Comparison shopping? These two photos reflect prices of food and clothing in the years 1920 and 1921. The latter was apparently the year for bargains in Sacramento.

The Kimball Upson Co.'s building at 609 K St. housed Sacramento's first radio station, KFBK which went on the air on September 23, 1922.

This is a photo of the newly completed Sutter General Hospital, built in the 1920s. Today, it is being remodeled to meet the needs of a rapidly growing community.

On July 1, 1925, at 4:10 p.m., the first air delivered mail arrived at Mather Field in Sacramento under the care of pilot Burr H. Winslow. Four thousand spectators were present for this historic event.

Mather Air Field, circa 1920. Today, Mather Field is one of the Air Force's major installations.

The D.W. Carmichael Real Estate Company owned large parcels of land east of Sacramento and sold them in five and ten acre lots in the 1920s. Today, this area of Sacramento county is the unincorporated city of Carmichael, a rapidly advancing suburb with many homes and businesses.

The interior of Fredericks Photo Service Company, June 17, 1926, according to the calendar on the wall at left.

First Straight Trainload of Onions
Ever Shipped From Sacramento
Forwarded by Wood Curtis Co..
Growers & Shippers. Sacramento, Calif.

Shipment of fruit and vegetables was a slow process at the turn of the century, yet, by 1927 an entire refrigerated trainload of onions was on its way east.

McCurry Foto Company has been in business for more than fifty years.

This aerial photo was taken in October of 1925.

This is a photo of one of two identical state office buildings that face each other just west of the capitol building. Built in the 1920s, they feature stone exteriors and oak, marble, and frescoe interiors.

This circa 1930 aerial view of the state capitol shows the enormity of the building and surrounding grounds.

The Ruhstaller Brewery, once one of Sacramento's most successful, stood ready for the wrecking crew in this circa 1930 photo.

The exterior of the Mohr and Yoerk butcher shop, circa 1930. The butcher shop occupied the first floor, and the other floors housed the offices of dentists, lawyers, and other professionals.

This interior of a Sacramento meat market shows the old-fashioned butcher at his best. Imagine paying twenty cents a pound for boneless prime rib!

The chorus line of a local vaudeville show poses with members of the Sacramento Police Department, circa 1930.

Hale Brothers Department Store, circa 1930.

J Street in the 1930s and the marquee of the State Theater. Vaudeville was a favorite form of entertainment. The State Theater and its neighbor, the Lyceum, have since closed their doors.

These five swimmers enjoy a dip in the Sacramento River under the I Street bridge. They are identified as, from the top, left to right: N. L. McCracken, L. Higgs, F. E. Peck, G. E. Miller, and E. J. Frickells.

Prize sheep pose with their proud owners during the California State Fair around 1930. Many exhibitors traveled hundreds of miles to show their livestock in the varied competitions.

154

Sacramento has many beautiful and challenging golf courses in the immediate area. These men pose for a group shot on a sunny 1930s afternoon at one of the many courses.

The Gospel Mission was a haven for men who were down on their luck. Here they could find shelter and occasional entertainment.

Y.M.C.A. Ranger
Christmas Dinner
1934

This little tyke, his face apparently done up in mock Indian war paint, does not look too pleased at his impending "scalping," but the barber seems fully prepared to give him a haircut.

This team of players were soccer champions in 1937 and 1938.

STATE CHAMPIONS 1937-38

The Sacramento YMCA hosted a Christmas dinner for these young gentlemen in 1934. The Y has always been active with youth groups as well as adult education and recreation.

K Street in the 1930s was crowded with automobiles, structures, and shoppers. A variety of quality stores made the street a popular thoroughfare.

The Sacramento Valley, one of the most fertile agricultural areas in the world, has many canning facilities. Libby's, Del Monte, and Campbell's Soups are among the many national brands that have been located in Sacramento. The Libby's plant is shown in the 1930s.

McCurry Foto

159

VINSON'S
BOOK STORE

Cantilever
Shoes

YANS
CANDIES

THE
SENATOR

CROWN
BILLIARDS

J Street after dark.

The Bank of America of California building stood on the corner of Seventh and J Street in this 1930s photo.

The corner of Second and K, circa 1930.

The E. W. Myers jewelry store at 724 K Street, shown about 1930, retailed jewelry and clocks and even provided eye examinations and glasses. This building offered one-stop shopping; upstairs you could also visit a dentist and have a permanent wave.

These men were members of the Sacramento Fire Department, Truck Number Three, Oak Park Station, in the 1930s: Captain L. C. Moore, Robert Russell France, Buck Campbell, Bang Bergland, Slim (Frank) Simons, Lester Foster, Charlie La Vine, and Marion Johnson.

Training flights over the downtown area were a startling sight. Sacramento appears to have been invaded in this 1930s picture showing air travel of the future as well as the slow-paced riverboats of the past.

These ladies pose for a group photo in the railroad yard. This was war time in Sacramento, a time for all to contribute to the country.

The Weinstock Lubin Company.

These aerial photos taken by David Joslyn depict Sacramento of the 1930s.

Almonds are of major importance to agriculture in California, and the Sacramento area
is surrounded by orchards
which harvest thousands of bins
per year. This 1940 photo, taken
in an almond orchard near
Orangevale in the northwest
portion of the county, was used
for a promotion by the California Almond Growers Association.

Sacramento swung its way through the Big Band Era.

GEORGIE BREECE
AND
HIS BAND

29818-7

The Ben Ali Band in full uniform is ready to perform in this photo taken at the Ben Ali temple, around 1940.

Tally-ho was a cry to be heard in the steeplechase class at the State Fair in the 1940s. These two unidentified riders jump a four-foot barrier in unison during a practice session before judging begins.

Ground breaking for the Bing Maloney Golf Course in September of 1950. This beautiful course is located on Freeport Boulevard adjacent to Sacramento Executive Airport.

Hart's Hamburger Joint was a popular spot for teenagers in the 1950s. There they could fill up on burgers, fries, milkshakes and all the rock-and-roll music they could stand from the juke box.

This young gentleman exhibits a fine steer in the 4-H class at the California State Fair. 4-H is much a part of young Sacramentans lives despite the apparent urban quality of living. Many groups are active throughout the area, some dealing with agriculture and some with more city-oriented projects.

Shakey's, a nationwide chain of pizza parlours, started in Sacramento. The franchise was founded by Shakey Johnson, who opened his first restaurant on May 5, 1954. The original Shakey's is still doing business at the corner of Fifth-Seventh and J streets. The Jockey Room, in the rear of the building, is still a popular "hangout," although members of the fairer sex are now welcomed.

Channel 40 broadcast from a tent during a State Fair in the 1950s.

KCCC channel 40 (now KXTL), Sacramento's VHF station, is the second largest independent television station in the country. Here, one of the station's first newsmen delivers his report.

Popular television personality Harry Martin was one of the first on the city's first station, KCCC Channel 40. Today, he hosts Weeknight, a nightly feature and entertainment series on KCRA, Channel 3.

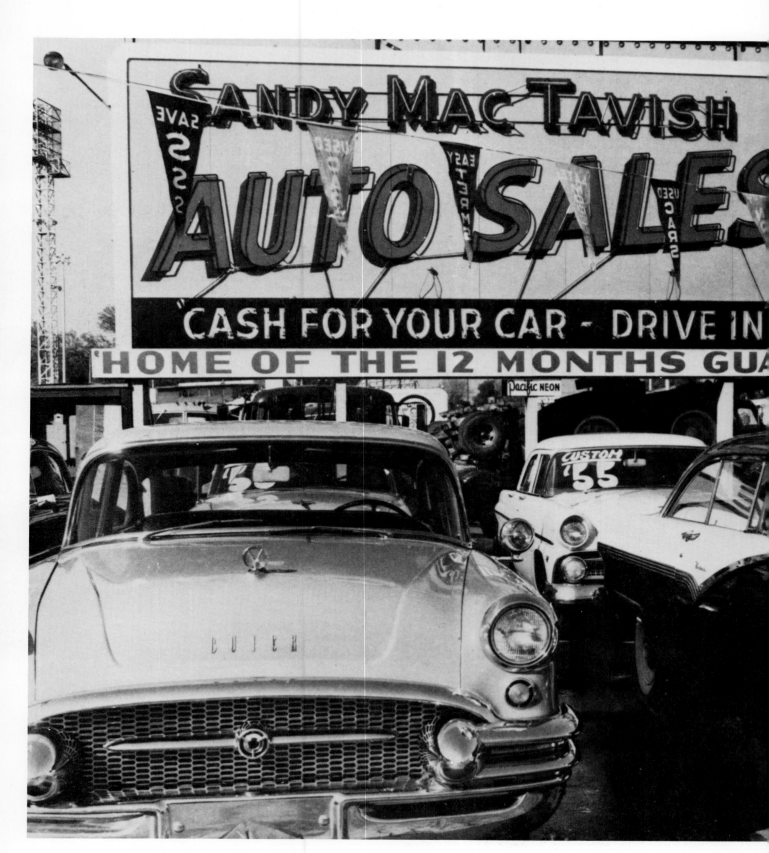

Garish car lot displays were as much a part of the 1950s as duck tails and poodle skirts.

Weinstock Lubin and the Senator Hotel circa 1950. Although the buildings still stand, both are being converted into office buildings.

Claus & Kraus Meats at the corner of Seventeenth and I streets has been in business since 1888. This early business, like many others in Sacramento, is still thriving today.

The Golden Eagle Hotel, a landmark to many Sacramentans,
fell beneath the wrecking ball in
the 1960s. Once a beautiful
example of the fashionable
hotel, in later years it had been
reduced to nearly a flop house
reputation. Built in the 1860s,
this fine hotel was a favorite of
visitors and was also a permanent residence for many Sacramentans during the last thirty
years of the nineteenth century.
The Golden Eagle could not
survive the advancing of technology and the accelerated
growth of the city.

Trinity Cathedral parish house (Episcopal) was razed in 1969 to make way for a new brick structure, the Cathedral House.

The Sacramento skyline looks much different today than in the past. Structures with character and style are either replaced or hidden from view by stark but efficient office buildings.

Today, St. Francis' Catholic Church is still on the original site of Twenty-Seventh and K streets, yet its stone edifice provides a striking contrast with the earlier facade.

Sacramento City Hall on the corner of Ninth and I streets.

Ronald Wilson Reagan, the fortieth president of the United States, was the twenty-ninth governor of California. Reagan, shown here dedicating the capitol buiding as a historical landmark, is a gifted speaker and eager campaigner whose distress over campus unrest and government interference with business led him to seek the governorship in the state's 1966 elections.

The one-time movie actor used the poise he gained on Hollywood's soundstages to help him project an image of a tough but likable leader. On November 8, 1966, Reagan, a Republican, defeated incumbent Democrat Edmund G. Brown by nearly a million votes. So eager was Reagan to pull in the reins on what he considered to be California's runaway government, that his swearing-in ceremony was held at midnight on inauguration day, January 2, 1967. He demonstrated early the sense of humor which became one of his trademarks. A few minutes after midnight, when his swearing-in was completed, Reagan turned to Senator George Murphy, himself a former movie actor, and said, "Well, George, here we are on the late show again."

During his eight years in Sacramento, Ronald Reagan may not have accomplished all that he would have liked to for the citizens of California, but he kept his honor intact. Reagan's diligence more than his accomplishments kept him popular with Californians. The qualities of leadership he demonstrates in Washington, D. C., were learned in the tough political arenas of Sacramento, California.

This photo accentuates the height of a California fan palm located in Capitol Park.

Capitol Park features an abundance of plants in forty acres of carefully maintained lawns and gardens which attract both tourists and residents. It is a beautiful area for quiet walks, picnic lunches, bicycling, or skating.

McKinley Park is a favorite spot for jogging, tennis, and a little fishing for the younger set. The site also houses a library, garden and art center, and a rose garden, where many local weddings are held. In the late nineteenth century this area was known as East Park. It was as popular then as it is today.

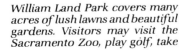

William Land Park covers many acres of lush lawns and beautiful gardens. Visitors may visit the Sacramento Zoo, play golf, take children to Fairytale town, or merely stroll through the area. It is a favorite area for softball and picnics also.

This photo of the Capitol shows the construction crane still in place. The building is undergoing comprehensive refurbishing. Detail to design and original style and material have been the concern of all who have worked on this major restoration.

Once a stopover for the elite and famous, the Senator Hotel has truly seen better days. Years of declining guests and financial trouble have taken their toll on this once-beautifully appointed structure. The hotel has been closed to await renovation and remodeling to accommodate the need for office space in the area adjacent to the Capitol building.

This brick structure covered with clinging vines was the home of the Libby's cannery for many years. It has closed its doors to the public but may soon be converted into a covered shopping area of fine shops and restaurants by local developers. It is an expansive building that would lend itself well to this new transition.

Weinstock's department store is located at Fifth and L streets in a new, contemporary building.

The facade is a striking arch of smoked glass which reflects the surroundings.

The Sacramento Community Center, located at Thirteenth and L streets in Sacramento, plays host to the Sacramento Symphony as well as to conventions, shows, and other attractions.

Five Mile Station at California State Univeristy, Sacramento, was a relay station for the Pony Express riders in 1860. The first rider heading eastward changed ponies on this site before continuing on toward St. Joseph, Missouri.

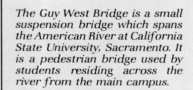

This high-rise structure at 555 Capitol Mall houses important local as well as national firms.

The building is enhanced by its distinctive fountain which is illuminated after dark.

The Guy West Bridge is a small suspension bridge which spans the American River at California State University, Sacramento. It is a pedestrian bridge used by students residing across the river from the main campus.

The Cathedral of the Blessed Sacrament today is surrounded by office and commercial buildings. Sacramento has grown up around this towering church, obscuring the grandeur of the architecture. Once a tall spire and dome on the skyline, now they are hidden by modern buildings.

The front door and statuary of the Cathedral of the Blessed Sacrament on the K Street Mall.

The Tower Theatre at Sixteenth and Broadway is a classic example of the neon era of advertising.

189

The Sacramento City Cemetery, located at Broadway and Riverside, is the burial place of many pioneers. The 1850 cholera epidemic took its toll on the city's residents, evidenced by the numerous tombstones with that date etched upon them. This cemetery is the final resting place for such notables as Mark Hopkins, co-founder of the Central Pacific Railroad, and Governors John Bigler, Newton Booth, and William Irwin.

These are the graves of John A. Sutter, Jr., the founder of the city, and Hardin Bigelow, the city's first mayor.

This aerial view of the downtown area of Sacramento was taken around 1963, before redevelopment began in earnest. The large Macy's department store was nearing completion in the center of the picture. Note the many vacant lots in the vicinity of the K Street Mall.

The family plot of the E. B. Crocker family located in the City Cemetery. E. B. and his wife Margaret are responsible for the famous Crocker Art Gallery, which houses some of the best western art as well as creations of modern and relatively new artists.

Cal-Expo is the site of the California State Fair. During fairtime, thousands of people crowd the grounds. Horseracing, rodeos, flower shows, and of course the midway are only a few of the attractions. The grounds and buildings are available year-round for other uses such as horse shows, dog shows, and sports shows. Lloyd Arnold's Golden Bear Raceway, a harness racing track, is in operation from May through August.

Sacramento is host to a world champion harness racer for the second time in this city's history. Warm Breeze, owned by Lloyd Arnold, paced to a record 1:53.1 on June 26, 1977, at Golden Bear Raceway.

Lloyd Arnold, executive director of Golden Bear Raceway, has entertained Sacramentans by offering fine harness racing to all in this area. The bettor and the casual fan enjoy the races in the spring of each year.

The Sacramento Savings and Loan building was the first commercial building constructed in a redevelopment area in the entire West. It was completed in March of 1962 at the corner of Fourth and L streets.

Governor Edmund G. Brown, father of Governor Jerry Brown, looks over a model of a proposed new fairground in January of 1963. The State Fair remained on Stockton Boulevard until 1970 when it opened on its new site on Exposition Boulevard on the American River.

Front Street on the embarcadero today appears much the same as it was 120 years ago. The restoration and reconstruction process have turned the largest skid row in California into a beautiful "park" from a bygone era.

Old Sacramento appeared somber and forlorn in the 1960s. The construction of the new freeway cut through the Old Town area, isolating it from the commercial district directly east. This area continued to deteriorate until the Sacramanto Redevelopment Agency stepped in to save these valuable structures.

Reconstruction and redevelopment continue in a never-ending project to enhance and beautify the area of Old Sacramento. Here bulldozers work on an alley between J and K streets between Front and Second.

Old Sacramento in the 1980s.

This aerial view of Sutter's Fort taken in the early 1960s shows the reconstruction of the inner buildings as well as the outside walls. St. Francis Catholic Church is visible above the trees behind the fort.

This striking white building was all that remained in the late nineteenth century of this once-important site. Today it is maintained by State Parks and Recreation, as is the entire area.

This building is on the north side of the grounds within the walls of the fort. Sutter and others operated a saloon, store, newspaper office and a hotel from this bastion of the frontier.

Sutter's Fort had been reduced to a shambles by the 1880s. It was hardly recognizable as the commerce center of the 1840s. The walls disappeared, leaving only a small pile of rubble, and the whitewashed main building was merely an eroded shell.

The reconstruction of Sutter's Fort began in 1891. Walls and buildings were constructed of original materials whenever possible. The area surrounding the fort was converted into a park which came under the jurisdiction of the state division of beaches and parks in 1947.

A local poet, Lucius Harwood Foote, expressed the general sentiment of those who gazed upon the ruins of the original fort in his poem, "Sutter's Fort."

SUTTER'S FORT

I stood by the old fort's crumbling wall,
*   On the eastern edge of the town;*
The sun through the clefts in the ruined hall
*   Flecked with its light the rafters brown.*

Charmed by the magic spell of the place,
*   The present vanished, the past returned,*
While rampart and fortress filled the space,
*   And yonder the Indian camp-fires burned.*

I heard the sentinels' measured tread,
*   The challenge prompt, the quick reply,*
I saw on the tower above my head
*   The Mexican banner flaunt the sky.*

Around me the waifs from every clime,
*   Blown by the fickle winds of chance,*
Knight errants, ready at any time
*   For any cause, to couch a lance.*

The staunch old Captain, with courtly grace,
*   Owner of countless leagues of land,*
Benignly governs the motley race,
*   Dispensing favors with open hand.*

Only a moment the vision came;
*   Where tower and rampart stood before,*
Where flushed the night with the camp's red flame,
*   Dust and ashes and nothing more.*

The Union building once housed the oldest daily newspaper in the west, the Sacramento Union. This paper is still in circulation today, but it is now located at Third and L streets and occupying an entire block. This photo depicts the reconstructed early building on J St. in Old Sacramento, now the Union Restaurant.

Bibliography

Bean, Walton. *California: An Interpretive History*. San Francisco: McGraw-Hill, 1978.

Clappe, L.A.K.S. (Dame Shirley). *The Shirley Letters from the California Mines, 1851-1852*. New York: Knopf, 1949.

Cook, Sherburne F. *The Conflict Between the California Indian and White Civilization*. Berkeley: Univ. of California Press, 1976.

Lord, Myrtle Shaw. *A Sacramento Saga*. Sacramento: Sacramento Chamber of Commerce, 1946.

McGowan, Joseph. *History of the Sacramento Valley*. New York: I. Lewis Historical Publishing, 1961.

Pitt, Leonard. *The Decline of the Californios: A Social History of the Spanish Speaking Californians, 1846-1890*. Berkeley: Univ. of California Press, 1966.

Sacramento Branch of the American Association of University Women. *Vanishing Victorians: A Guide to the Historic Homes of Sacramento*. 1973.

Severson, Thor. *Sacramento: An Illustrated History, 1839-1874, from Sutter's Fort to Capital City*. San Francisco: California Historical Society, 1973.

Teacher, Lawrence, ed. *The Unabridged Mark Twain*. Vol. 2. Philadelphia: Running Press, 1979.

Wright, Louis B. *Life on the American Frontier*. New York: Putnam, 1971.

Index

A

Adams Express Company,   27
Agricultural fair,   28
Agricultural Pavilion,   97
Agriculture,   67, 169
Alaska,   16
Alvarado (Mexican governor),   17
American River,   13, 14, 16, 17, 95, 100, 188, 193
Anchor Bakery,   135
Anspach Mule Company,   64
Antelope,   54
Apache,   55
Arnold, Lloyd,   192
Artful Dodger,   42
Associated Order of Foresters of America,   86

B

Babson, Seth,   70
Bank of America of California,   162
Bell Conservatory,   74
Ben Ali band,   172
Ben Ali temple,   172
Bergland, Bang,   164
Bigelow, Hardin,   191
Bigler, John,   191
"Black Bart,"   28
Bloomer Cut,   38
Boles, Charles ("Black Bart"),   28
Booth, Newton,   191
Boulevard Park,   95
Brannan, Sam,   23
Breweries,   58, 59, 67, 75, 148
    Buffalo Brewery,   75
    Ruhstaller's City Brewery,   58, 59, 148
Brown, Edmund G.,   184, 193
Brown, Jerry,   193
Bruener, John,   32, 97
Bruener, John, Company (department store),   31, 32, 102
Buffalo Brewery,   75
Butler, A. G.,   94

C

California Almond Growers Association,   169
California Museum Association,   107
California Stage Company,   29, 30
California State Agricultural Society,   95
California State Exposition grounds,   95, 192
California State Fair,   92-93, 95-98, 136, 154, 172, 175, 192-193
California State Park & Recreation Department,   72, 201
California State University,   188
California Steam Navigation Company,   53, 54, 55
Campbell, Buck,   164
Campbell's Soups,   158
Capitol building,   46, 48, 49, 146, 147, 186

Capitol City Wheelmen,   88
Capitol Commission,   72
Capitol Gas Company,   97
Capitol Park,   75, 185
Carmichael (town),   144
Carmichael, D. W., Real Estate Company,   144
Cassidy, Barry,   11
Cathedral House,   182
Cathedral of the Blessed Sacrament,   35, 189
Central Pacific Hospital,   74
Central Pacific Railroad,   28, 38, 40, 42, 44, 45, 70, 74, 89, 95, 108, 191
Chin Du Wan,   54
China Camp,   24
China Slough,   108
Chinatown,   137
Chinese Baptist chapel,   34
Chinese laborers,   41
Chinese miners,   24
Chinese people,   34
Chop Suey Cafe,   137
Chrysopolis,   53, 54
"City of the Plain,"   13
Citizen's Fire Committee,   100
City Cemetery,   190, 191
Civil War,   41, 49, 75
Claus & Kraus Meats,   180
Coloma (town),   17, 22, 23
Consumnes,   57
Corbett, H. W.,   29
Crocker Art Gallery,   107, 190
Crocker, Charles,   40, 41, 70
Crocker, E. B.,   107, 190
Crocker, Margaret,   74, 106, 107, 190
Crosby, Bing,   51
Cumberland Coal Company,   28
Curtis Park,   94

D

Del Monte,   158
Delta King,   56, 132
Delta Queen,   56
"Dixie,"   51

E

Eagle Theatre,   23
East Park,   185
Egl, Anthony,   33
Elk Grove Park,   83
Ellsworth, William,   60

F

Farley, S. H.,   63
Fashion Stables,   85

Fat City, 24
Fat, Frank, 24
Fire, 17, 18, 100
"First house," 15
Five Mile Station, 188
Floods, 17, 30, 48, 49, 82
Foote, Lucius Harwood, 202
Foster, Lester, 164
Fredericks Photo Service Company, 134, 144
Fremont Primary School, 115
Frickells, E. J., 153
France, Robert Russell, 164

G
Gambling, 26
Gallatin, Albert, 72, 73
Gilt Edge Baseball Club, 59
Gilt Edge Beer, 59
Glen Dairy, 57
Gold, 17, 19, 22-26, 47
Golden Bear Raceway, 192
Golden Eagle Dairy, 82
Golden Eagle Hotel, 181
Golden Gate Park, 74
Goodell, N. D., 72
Gospel Mission, 155
Governor Stanford (locomotive), 42
Grant, Ulysses, 74
Guy West Bridge, 188

H
Haggin, James Ben Ali, 85, 113
Hale Brothers Department Store, 152
Harte, Bret, 26
Hart's Hamburger Joint, 174
Hastings Building, 37
Higgs, L., 153
Hollywood, 184
Holmes, Morey, 70
Hopkins, Mark, 40, 191
Hotel Land, 137
Hotel St. James, 138
Hotels
    Golden Eagle, 181
    Land, 137
    Orleans, 94
    St. James, 138
    Senator, 130, 180, 186
    Western, 102
Hungary, 33
Huntington, Collis P., 40, 41
Huntington Hopkins hardware store, 28, 72
Huntington, Miss (school principal), 115

I
Indians, 13, 14, 17, 25
Irwin, William, 191

J
Japanese-Americans, 113
John Bruener Company, 31, 32, 102
Johnson, Marion, 164
Johnson, Myrtle, 110
Johnson, Shakey, 175
Joslyn, David, 166
"Joyland," 116
Judah, T. D., 38, 40, 41

K
KCRA, 177
KFBK, 142
Kimball Upson Company, 142
Kidd, Captain, 53
Knights of Pythias, 87
KXTL (KCCC), 176, 177

L
La Grange, 30
La Vine, Charlie, 164
Land, William, Park, 185
Libby's, 158, 186
Liberty Iron Works, 124
"Long Tom," 25
Louisiana race course, 94, 95
Lyceum Theater, 152

M
MacBride, Kirt, 138
Maidu Indians, 13, 17
Majors, Alexander, 36
Maloney, Bing Golf Course, 173
Marala, George, 103
Marala, J. Calvert, 103
Marala, Joyce, 103
Marala, Oliver, 103
Marshall, James W., 22, 23
Martin, Harry, 177
Marty and Brothers, 82
Marty, Tony, 82
Masonic Lodge, 86
Mather Air Field, 113, 124, 143
McCracken, N. L., 153
McCurry's Foto Company, 145
McCurry's Photo Lab, 11
McGowan, Joseph A., 100
McKinley Park, 185
Mexican authorities, 17
Miller, G. E., 153
Miners' Variety Store, 25
Mission Dolores, 95
Mohr and Yoerk butcher shop, 148
Monterey, 17, 18
Moore, L. C., 164
Moraga, Gabriel, 17
Mountain ranges
    Pacific Coast, 13
    Sierra Nevada, 13, 28, 38, 41
Murphy, George, 184
Myers, E. W., jewelry store, 162

N
Negro Bar, 38
Nevada, 53
New Helvetia, 16, 22
Newspapers
    Sacramento Bee, 75
    Sacramento Union, 123, 138
New World, 53
New York, 23
Nielsen, J. M., 61
Noacks Jewelry Store, 62
North Sacramento, 113, 124

O
Oak Park, 63, 116

Oak Park Gateway, 116
Oak Park School, 76
Oak Park Station, 164
Occident, 95
Odd-Fellows Bank, 94
"Old Corner" bar, 60
"Old Diamond," 88
"Old Leakers" Baseball Club, 79
Opposition Steamship Line, 54
Orangevale, 81, 169
Orleans Hotel, 94

P
Pacific Coast Mountain Range, 13
Pacific Mutual Life Insurance Company, 61
Pacific Railroad, 12
Pearl Harbor, 113
Peasley, John, 96
Peck, F. E., 153
Pioneer Society, 74
Pioneer Telegraph Building, 61
Plaza Park, 45
Ponner, A. J., sewing machine, 97
Pony Express, 36-37, 188
Pullman Strike of 1894, 88
Pythian Castle, 87

Q

R
Railroads, 81, 40
    Central Pacific, 28, 38, 40, 42, 44, 45, 70, 74, 89, 95, 108, 191
    Pacific, 12
    Sacramento Valley, 38
    Southern Pacific, 34, 90, 91, 108, 111, 118, 128, 129, 169
    Union Pacific, 42
Rancho Del Paso, 85, 113
Reagan, Ronald Wilson, 184
Reese, Uriah, 72
Rhoads School, 83
Richard, Miss (teacher), 115
Rio Linda, 113
Riverboats
    Antelope, 54
    Apache, 55
    Chin Du Wan, 54
    Chrysopolis, 53, 54
    Delta King, 56, 132
    Delta Queen, 56, 132
    Nevada, 53
    New World, 53
    Washoe, 53
    Yosemite, 53
Rivers, 32, 82
    American, 13, 14, 16, 17, 95, 100, 188, 193
    Sacramento, 13, 14, 16, 17, 19, 23, 47, 51, 53, 100, 153
Ruhstaller's City Brewery, 58, 59, 148
Russell, William, 36

S
Sacramento Bee, 75
Sacramento City Cemetery, 190, 191
Sacramento City Hall, 184
Sacramento Common School District, 83
Sacramento Community Center, 187
Sacramento County Courthouse, 48, 120
Sacramento Executive Airport, 173

Sacramento Fire Department, 139, 164
Sacramento High School, 119, 122
Sacramento Historical Society, 11
Sacramento Memorial Auditorium, 84, 126
Sacramento Park Association, 95
Sacramento Police Department, 138, 151
Sacramento Redevelopment Agency, 114, 196
Sacramento River, 13, 14, 16, 17, 19, 23, 47, 51, 53, 100, 153
Sacramento Symphony, 187
Sacramento Union, 123, 138
Sacramento Valley, 12, 15, 158
Sacramento Valley Railroad, 38
Sacramento YMCA, 157
Sacramento Zoo, 185
Saint Francis Catholic Church, 34, 183, 200
Saint Rose of Lima Catholic Church, 34
Sandwich Islands, 16
San Jose, 18
Seadler, James, 70
Sells-Floto Circus, 117
Senator Hotel, 130, 180, 186
Severson, Thor, 28
Shakey's, 175
Sierra Nevada Mountain Range, 13, 28, 38, 41
Silver Grey, 94
Simons, Slim (Frank), 164
Sisters of Mercy Hospital, 74
Skaggs, E. M., 94
Sloughhouse, 106, 115
Southern Baptists of Virginia, 34
Southern Pacific Railroad, 34, 90, 91, 108, 111, 118, 128, 129, 169
Stanford, Leland, 40, 69, 95
State Agricultural Pavilion, 94
State Fair, 92, 93, 95, 96, 97, 98, 136, 154, 172, 175, 192, 193
State Theater, 152
Steamboat, 23
Steffens, Joseph, 72
Steffens, Lincoln, 72
Stevens, A. J., 45
Sunset Telephone Company, 112
Sutter General Hospital, 142
Sutter, John A. (Johan Augustus), 16, 17, 22, 23, 201
Sutter, John A., Jr., 18, 191
Sutter's Fort, 19, 36, 200-202
"Sutter's Fort," 202
Sutter's Lake, 108
Sutter's Mill, 22

T
Thomson-Diggs Company, 55
Tower Theatre, 189
Tractor, steam-propelled, 47
Transcontinental telegraph, 36
Trinity Cathedral (Episcopal), 182
Twain, Mark, 12, 36

U
Union Pacific Railroad, 42
Union Park, 95, 136
Union Primary School, 79
United States Air Force, 143
United States Post Office, 34, 105

V
VanVoorhies, A. A., 33

W

W. and O. Pharmacy,   137
Waddell, W. B.,   36
Warm Breeze,   192
Warner, William H.,   18
Warren's New England Seed Store,   28
Washington, D.C.,   184
Washoe,   53
Watson, Mary J., Grammar School,   84, 126
Weinstock and Lubin Company,   31, 97, 165, 180, 187
Wells Fargo,   27, 33, 65
Western Hotel,   102
What Cheer House,   96
White House,   18
Williams, Llewellyn,   70
Winslow, Burr H.,   143
World War I,   113, 118, 124
World War II,   113

X

Y

Yardley, H. Edward,   70
Yerba Buena (San Francisco),   17
YMCA,   157
Yosemite,   53
Young America Volunteer Fire Company,   99
Young Tecumseh,   96
Y Street Dairy,   63